THE
FORBIDDEN
SELF

THE
FORBIDDEN
SELF

*Symbolic Incest
and the Journey Within*

J O H N   P E R K I N S

S H A M B H A L A
Boston & London
1992

Shambhala Publications
Horticultural Hall
300 Massachusetts Avenue
Boston, Massachusetts 02115

9 8 7 6 5 4 3 2 1
First Edition
Printed in the United States of America on acid-free paper ∞
Distributed in the United States by Random House, Inc., and in Canada
by Random House of Canada Ltd

Library of Congress Cataloging-in-Publication Data

Perkins, John, 1939–
The forbidden self: symbolic incest and the journey within/
John Perkins.—1st ed.
p.   cm.
Includes bibliographical references.
ISBN 0-87773-871-8
1. Symbolism (Psychology)   2. Individuation (Psychology)
I. Title.
BF175.5.S95P47   1993   92-50440
155.2—dc20   CIP

To the memory of
JOSEPH A. ROPER
(1908–1989)

Your vision will become clear only when you can look into your own heart. . . . Who looks outside, dreams; who looks inside, awakes. — C . G . JUNG

There are two ways to life: One is the regular, direct, and good way; the other is bad, it leads through death, and that is the way of genius. — THOMAS MANN

It was the stone rejected by the builders that proved to be the keystone; this is Yahweh's doing and it is wonderful to see.
— PSALM 118 : 2 2 – 2 3

CONTENTS

◆

FOREWORD

◆

SEVERAL years ago during a trip to India I made friends with a
Brahman priest named Sundaramoorthy. He was thirty years old
but looked twenty. He was always smiling. He is the son, grand-
son, great-grandson of priests to Nataraja Shiva as far back as the
mind can imagine. Slender, quick, highly intelligent, Sundaramoorthy is the happiest man I have ever known. He knows
nothing of the modern world, and he is the only grown man I have
ever met who is still a citizen of the Garden of Eden. No time
pressure, worry, or self-consciousness has ever crossed that serene face. He has an aristocracy of spirit unknown to me before
my meeting with him.

Up until the Middle Ages mankind enjoyed this simple way of
living in which dream, imagination, and ceremonies enacting
the sacredness of cosmic events did not conflict with the literal
truth we now prefer. Man trusted a reality greater than himself, the transpersonal powers, without question. Our earlier,
innocent musing was the poetry of living. The world was
(and still is in some regions like parts of India) a filthy,
dangerous, and disease-ridden place, and yet people were probably far happier, more at home in the universe, and more at
peace with themselves back then than they are in our own
times.

Beginning with the European Middle Ages, another level
of consciousness gradually arose. Man began to conceive of
himself—instead of God—as the center of life's universal

drama. Put in psychological terms, man gave birth to a personal ego consciousness from the Gothic through the Renaissance period, and the "fairy tales" that inspired earlier ancestors steadily began to disappear as serious depictions of truth. Now we have reality. We're grown up and have the facts. We've got something to think about and something to worry about.

The tragic neurosis of our day is that we have lost our childhood. The worrisome mark of this loss can be found carved into the faces of most Western people beyond the age of forty.

Many people who have come into my analytic practice over the years had achieved success and recognition, but they remained unhappy, strangely unfulfilled. Something gnawed at them.

Unhappy people often attempt to storm the gates of Eden and climb back into the bliss of childhood innocence. They try to recapture the ecstasy of childlike abandon by indulging in drugs or rushing into compulsive sex, or they may attempt in countless ways to contrive the illusion of rustic simplicity, whimsical spontaneity, or spiritual serenity. These are the "laid-back" people.

But too much of this appears to be merely an infantile and sentimental escape. It is a charade that does no justice at all to genuine childlikeness or true devotion. It has been aptly put that "you can't go home again."

A modern adult can't innocently return to childhood pure and simple. He or she must pass through a series of difficult death-and-rebirth experiences, each of which is a stage of psychological transformation along the path to achieving wholeness and a new, evolved sense of well-being.

In *The Forbidden Self*, John Perkins masterfully shows the pitfalls in life that ensnare and imprison us before we can graduate to a new state of rapture that is no longer childish but enlightened.

Like Parsifal or Don Quixote, the hero of the fascinating yet gravely disturbing tale that Mr. Perkins interprets is a fool. He is even a criminal fool. But in the very end he becomes a sagacious and a truly magnificent one. He reveals to us the promise of our redemption—our attaining to psychic and spiritual completeness. Thank God. May he live within us!

ROBERT A. JOHNSON

ACKNOWLEDGMENTS

◆

The late T. S. Matthews launched the immediate process that led to this book by graciously presenting me with my first copy of Thomas Mann's playfully grave little novel *The Holy Sinner*.

Richard Hadden, Sally Keil, and Elizabeth Winthrop read the manuscript in depth and made crucial editorial suggestions. Brewster Beach, Winifred Clark, and Grenville Cuyler also made valuable contributions. Without the counsel of these excellent and dedicated friends, this work could never have reached the point of publication. My editor at Shambhala, Emily Hilburn Sell, has given my manuscript the benefit of her keen judgment, warm appreciation, and confident enthusiasm. Kendra Crossen applied her legendary abilities to the meticulous task of copy editing, for which I am exceedingly grateful.

Of great assistance to me concerning the trauma of incestuous child abuse were the cogent insights and comments of Anne Elizabeth Connor and Carolyn Slaughter.

Most of all I am indebted to my indefatigable and irrepressible bride, Margery S. Cuyler, herself a writer and editor, for her professional guidance and especially for her generous love, her unflagging moral support, and her relentless faith in my ability to accomplish this task.

On the very eve of publication, I take pride in celebrating thirty years of guidance, inspiration, and friendship in collaboration with my spiritual father, Robert A. Johnson. His extraordinary presence, ruthless honesty, mischievous wit, outrageous enthusiasm, and noble generosity have unfailingly attended me since our first encounter on a cold Michigan day at St. Gregory's Priory. *Aurum nostrum non est aurum vulgi.* "Our gold is not the common gold."

FEBRUARY 15, 1993

THE
FORBIDDEN
SELF

INTRODUCTION

♦

THE lives of our early ancestors were imbedded in the ground of myth. Imagination, dream, and folktale presented these people with everything they knew about the surrounding world and its origin. From myth they learned of the eternally validated shape and function of the cosmos and of society, and about the unfolding course of human development from birth to death and beyond. They lived down into the very core of their being through their myths, and through the ceremonial rituals by which these myths were reenacted from day to day and from season to season.

To people of archaic times, myths were not cleverly devised theories invented to explain the hows and whys of life. They were simply the obvious facts of existence, which touched the very soul. These facts gave their lives meaning and purpose, and enabled them to live at home in a familiar world with secure fulfillment and a splendid satisfaction of the heart.

"After all," remarked the chief of the Taos Pueblos to Dr. Carl Gustav Jung during his 1925 visit to New Mexico, "we are a people who live on the roof of the world; we are the sons of Father Sun, and with our religion we daily help our father to go across the sky. We do this not only for ourselves, but for the whole world. If we were to cease practicing our religion, in ten years the sun would no longer rise. Then it would be night forever."[1]

Modern science has demonstrated that such mythic ways of

thinking are technically incorrect. However, the depth psychologists, particularly Jung, have shown that the symbols of myth and ritual are indeed profound truths about our inner life. It is only the *language* of myth that is fictional. The messages that such symbolic terms convey to us are the veritable *facts* of the psyche.

It has been a great disservice to humanity that some modern "enlightened" folk have so cavalierly dismissed the age-old forms of myth as mere childish superstition or illusion. This presumptuous devaluation of myth could not be further from the truth. Such "illusions" are positively life-sustaining to any traditional society, and the trivialization of a people's mythology by more "civilized" white Europeans has wrenched the very heart and soul from that people, casting them adrift on a sea of alienation, meaninglessness and despair.

"Myth," said Jung, "is the revelation of a divine life in man."[2] Without an experience of this vital energy, which runs through the whole of the cosmos, and to which some mysterious presence within us both responds and corresponds, no human being could endure. For his or her existence would become hollow, a shell of the life once lived long ago. There would be no purpose, no mystery, no awe or rapture. Instead there would be a merely dead and artless existence, gripped by the idolatry of a concrete literal-mindedness, "Waiting for Godot."

When Jung had finished his stay among the Native Americans in New Mexico, he traveled back to Switzerland with a profound sense of awe and respect for the first indigenous nonwhite non-Europeans he had ever met. It was only then that Jung began to realize that our Western culture suffers a much greater poverty of soul than the Pueblos. Through our rationalistic enlightenment, we have increasingly lost our myth, and that is why so much of the enchantment and thrill of living have departed from our midst. We have made impressive gains in technology and in material prosperity, but it has cost us dearly. Our myth, which enfolded us like an inspiring guardian angel, has deserted us. A truly ecstatic rapture of the heart is an ever more rare experience for the adult person today.

Somewhere deep within, many of us have a gnawing sense that the Pueblos were right. If we finally lose psychological contact with our spiritual source, an eternal night will indeed descend upon our souls. It is happening already. We call it "alienation," "depression," and "ennui."

The mythic tale that this book examines has a long history. Its roots lie far back in the ancient Near East. Later it surfaced in classical Greece in the form of Sophocles' dramas about the legendary King Oedipus. Another version circulated in North Africa during the fifth century A.D. Then in twelfth-century southern France this epic was sung again by the troubadours. Within a generation, it was set to metrical stanzas, first in the language of Provençal and then by the Middle High German poet Hartmann von Aue, who entitled it *Gregorius von Stein*, that is, "Gregory of the Rock." It is the translation by Sheema Zeben Buehne, entitled *Gregorius: The Good Sinner*, upon which the present retelling and interpretation are based.[3]

In 1951, the Nobel Prize–winning German novelist Thomas Mann published the latest incarnation of this story. He called it *Der Ehrvelte*, or "The Chosen One," which appeared simultaneously in English as *The Holy Sinner*.[4]

Mann once said of *The Holy Sinner* to a journalist-critic, "In all immodesty I can say that with this work I have brought something new into German literature, something unique in itself and therefore unrepeatable. . . . It seems to me as if nothing like this will come again. Often our contemporary literature, the highest and the finest of it, appears like a farewell, an ephemeral remembrance . . . a calling back and a re-capturing of the Occidental mythos, before the night sings, a long night perhaps, and a deep forgetting. A little work like this is late culture, which comes before barbarism."[5]

Mann viewed our capacity to experience the vital pulse of great mythic literature as increasingly restricted. He felt that an ancient story like the Gregory tale, which had enjoyed such a long and varied history, could scarcely be told again, because modern readers lack the authentic spiritual innocence to resonate with it. Mann believed that the religious core expressed in the Gregory tale had already been eclipsed by the profane secularity of our declining civilization.

If Mann was right, we may now have only a final, fleeting opportunity to glimpse the significance of our spiritual heritage as we enter a new dark age of estrangement from the mythic ground. Our collective memory of living participation in the wisdom of great legends is rapidly fading from our consciousness, and is irrelevant to the vulgar cast of our present-day temporality. This depressing circumstance makes our Gregory tale all the more vital for our awareness today, if we hope to maintain even the slenderest connection to our spiritual source and thereby comprehend the sublime scope of human experience.

On a brighter note, perhaps the present resurgence of interest in mythology and depth psychology will open a new approach to the mythic foundations of our existence. For this is a tale about and for ourselves, a kind of X-ray picture of part of our spiritual heritage. It illuminates certain vital events that have been taking place within the personality and culture of Europeans, and that must be completed and fulfilled in us as we reach the close of this great millennial period in our history.

"Myths are public dreams," said Joseph Campbell, "and dreams are private myths."[6] Just as the great mythic tales reflect the comparative anatomy of a whole culture's psychology, so do the nocturnal images that visit us during sleep depict the shape of the individual psyche.

Today, there are an increasing number of individuals whose "private myths" intersect with the big "public dreams." For such people, a great mythic story from the past, particularly one from so pivotal a period as the twelfth century, may serve as an invaluable guide to psychological development. Individual potential may be appreciated and measured against a backdrop of the greater drama of an overall psychological evolution.

It was in the twelfth century that much of the psychological groundwork was laid for our era. The mythic folklore and literature from this period may function as a treasure map for the up-to-date explorer of the modern personality. Our tale succinctly demonstrates how the seeds of our growing individual consciousness were first planted by our Gothic forebears eight centuries ago, and how this incipient development both excited and deeply troubled our even earlier ancestors a millennium or two before that.

How can this centuries-old story from medieval times be of relevance today? It was Jung who carried the study of mythic symbolic forms to new depths of appreciation through developing his model of the archetypes of the collective unconscious.

According to Jung, these archetypes are the building blocks of the psyche, composing the structure, though not the actual content, of our psychological experience. In general outline, the archetypes govern the way we experience and respond to the episodes of life.

The irresistibly charming man or woman with whom we fall in love, the enemy who provokes fear or courage in our heart, or that indescribably beautiful panorama of mountains, ocean, or sky is transmitted to our consciousness with a built-in interpretation and value. Just as the eye apprehends light, so the archetypal images within the structure of the psyche reckon and formulate for us an experience of the environment. [7]

The images of water, light, sky, sun, moon, stars, rain, lightning, man, woman, mother, father, hero, child, cave, tree, wise crone, rat, wolf, buffalo, bear, snake, fish, eagle—all the perennial and universal experiences of human life on this earth have left their residue within the psyche. In a kind of rough general pattern, we are prepared to encounter the manifold elements and events of our environment in a characteristically human way. The shape of nature and the stellar cosmos resonates within the human soul and is not merely an external experience. Apparently, evolution has made it so.

Like a seed, which contains the developmental program of the fully mature tree within its genetic code, so the archetypal psyche intuits the larger and typical challenges that lie ahead in both the life of the individual and the history of any culture. This is no speculation regarding some magic power of prognostication. Such a prophetic insightfulness is simply an indication that the origin, growth, flowering, and end of cultures, as well as of individual lives, are influenced largely by the same factors shared by all mankind.

Jung employed the term *individuation* to describe the path along which the personality travels as it grows toward wholeness and greater consciousness. Jung does not use this term to indicate a penchant for egoistic eccentricity. Rather, *individuation* suggests the gradual unfolding of a greater and deeper integrity of the "Self." This process brings to realization a person's entire human nature in such a manner that realistic and healthy relations with others are increased, and delusion and isolation are overcome. The word *individual* really means "nondividable" and suggests wholeness and integrity rather than a narcissistic striving to be "different." Individuation is the growth of that special and unique Being deep inside each of us that is beyond ego, so that our lives may be lived responsibly in creative interaction with other individuals, and not dependently, or derivatively, according to the prejudices of the herd.

The process of individuation often begins with a circumstance that is generally beyond a person's control or devising. What is typically experienced is a certain dislocation or alienation from the average or "normal" program of living. One encounters an inner resistance (which is often misinterpreted as failure or inferiority) to the success styles of living that have been ingrained from childhood. How often has a middle-aged person consulted me with the complaint that he or she feels empty and depressed, even though outwardly successful in work and marriage.

The resistance may first appear as a nagging sense of inferiority or self-doubt, as simply an amorphous malaise or depression, or as a steadily increasing dissatisfaction with those forms of success that "ought" to prove rewarding and fulfilling, but simply don't. Somewhere from deep within emerges the feeling that, in the words of Henry David Thoreau, one "marches to the step of a different drummer."

If this discomfort is simply a complaint about a lack of social esteem or an inability to compete successfully, then it is an episode of ego inflation that does not in the least herald the advent of true individuation. At this level it is merely a childish wish to have one's cravings satisfied.

Individuation rarely develops in the lives of those who may seek counseling merely because of an "interest" in psychological matters, or to "understand" themselves. Nor does it appear in those who in other ways seek "enrichment" or attempt to "maximize their potential." The real hallmarks of individuation are a genuine and often fearful questioning of one's attitudes, values, and goals, and a real suffering of conflict, dislocation, and confusion. As the old scriptural saying advises, one must indeed lose one's life in order to find it.[8]

During the formative years our personalities develop in a somewhat one-sided fashion, suppressing many natural inclinations or variations that do not fit into the culture's ingrained program for living. Later, as we begin to realize that wholeness and completeness are more important than the perfect attainment of those ideals, a new opportunity is opened to us.

When I was a child, I was given a coloring book filled with pictures of different kinds of trees with separate drawings of the leaves proper to each tree. But when I collected some leaves from actual trees, these never matched the drawings in the book except in a very general way. Each live leaf was different from every other, and from the schematic drawing. The picture in the book was an ideal shape for each species of tree, but it simply did not exist in reality. There was no such thing as a "perfect" leaf except as the somewhat abstract design in the book presented it.

We are like those live leaves, not the idealized depictions. When we begin to focus on our actual personality, on its natural integrity, and not so much on the schematic expectation of how we "ought" to be as people, then we have a chance to reclaim all of those left-out elements of our personality and character. This involves coming to terms with our "shadow" sides, aspects of us which have remained ignored, undeveloped, or purposefully suppressed by the prejudice of our ideal strivings.

Suddenly, we may crave to explore artistic yearnings or try different partners or travel to exotic locales. A restlessness seizes our souls. At this point in our lives it is important to realize that *experience* and *expression* are generally not the same thing at all. A person may throw everything over, go off somewhere to a romantic new life, leaving all the familiar things and persons behind, but still not accomplish anything. One may act it all out, but still not suffer the experience of integration; one will have merely exchanged one form of lopsidedness for another. The responsible and devoted family man or woman stands to gain nothing from suddenly becoming a starry-eyed and free-spirited libertine. One should acknowledge one's shadow, not be possessed by it or simply flaunt it.

Our most important task is to integrate the various sides of our lives, not substitute one for the other. What we previously considered either inferior or negative in our character may then be reevaluated in such a way that we can make a connection with this shadow side, and thereby enormously augment the scope of our consciousness. The shadow is that part of our whole personality that has been excluded by our need to conform to the values and behavioral traits of our family and culture. This part, which seems incompatible with the "good" person we are supposed to be, is jettisoned into the unconscious, where it continues to make trouble in our fantasies, impulses, and relations with other people.

Making peace with the shadow causes a major change in the conscious point of view. We learn to make numerous adjustments and allowances in relation to our previous ideal values, and this brings our mentality more down to earth in ordinary reality. Much valuable self-acceptance and peace of mind result from this.

When the conscious outer personality has been reconstituted sufficiently through integration with various shadow elements, it is then possible to shift into an entirely new level of psychological development. This stage concerns the strictly *inner* personality, which is not part of our normal gender identification in the world. According to Jung, we all have an inner partner of the opposite sex, the masculine *animus* aspect of a woman's personality, or the feminine *anima* part of a man's psyche.[9] These are the two primary archetypal elements of human nature.

The animus or the anima is the personification of everything inside us that is unconscious, strange, and mysterious. They each represent the "other half" of our psychological makeup. Each appears commonly in our dreams as a person of the opposite sex with whom we have a compelling but generally problematic relationship. To the degree that we are unacquainted with these sides of ourselves, in outer life we will invariably experience them in projection to someone of the opposite sex. Then our relations with those other people will be disturbed, and charged with volatile emotions. We will lack objectivity and be carried away by the surge of either loathing or romance.

A successfully direct *interior* relation to the animus or anima produces a rare type of inner satisfaction and fulfillment. The person feels more complete and whole in his or her self, and there is a marked lessening of irrational moods, bossy opinions, and compulsive behavior. Evidence of a successful relation to anima or animus is a more consistently level mood without sudden periodic upheavals, a calmer acceptance of life, much less of a tendency to measure oneself in comparison to others, and a peculiar inner joy that whispers, "I'm my own self, I'm O.K. as I am, and I am living my own life." Those who have come to terms with these inner partners seem to know how to truly acknowledge and respect themselves and love other people. They are far more capable of individual judgment and discretion than is commonly encountered among collective-minded humanity. They are much more capable of genuinely intimate relationships.

One of the central themes of this book is our need to integrate the masculine and feminine halves of the psyche in our lives. The traditional perfectionistic patriarchal culture has consistently attempted to morally subdue and coerce the realm of nature and impulse toward its own idealistic ends. The impulses of the human heart and body, together with the intimacy of spontaneous relatedness between persons, have been trampled under this absolute authority. If there was any real connection between the realms of nature and spirit, of masculine and feminine energies in our civilization, it was certainly a very one-sided marriage. This book concerns the balancing of masculine and feminine polarity, to form a wholeness of life and experience.

The final stage of individuation consists in an increasing shift of emphasis away from the exterior personality and ego-centered consciousness to an inner spiritual center. This is often more marked in the second half of life, when people are more likely to "mellow out," but there are exceptional instances in young people as well.

This new center Jung called the Self, which he understood to be an inner, non-ego equivalent of the immanent image of God in the human soul. This center of wholeness and transcendent power carries one's life beyond the confines of familial, local, or ethnic programs of living. It provides an unshakable, rocklike foundation that is unthreatened by the opposites of fear and desire, personal inclination and duty, good and evil, life and death, or time and eternity. This acultural standpoint consists of a deeper level of wisdom and capacity for rapturous experience that are associated with ultimate questions of meaning and purpose in existence.

Traditional expressions of this stage are the wise saints and holy people whose lives are centered, for instance, on the inner Christ, the hidden buddha-nature, or the *atman-purusha* of Hinduism. At this stage, in a certain sense, one is no longer living one's own life, but Life itself is living uniquely through one's own more limited being. This is not a matter of belief, but of actual living experience.

Another major theme of this book is the psychology of incest. Depth psychology has demonstrated that there are two levels of incest. One is inner, symbolic, and potentially creative; the other, outer, literal, concrete, and destructive. One level can be the interior process of psychological integration, the "becoming one with the deeper Self"—a spiritual phenomenon of wholeness and holiness—that does not belong within *any* interpersonal relationship. The other level of incest is the pathological acting out or displacement of this archetypal integration to the arena of family relations, especially those between parent and child and between siblings.

The horrible violation, devastation, and psychological pollution that actual incest causes in the lives of helpless children results from the fragmentation, debasement, and compulsive projection of the Self, the divine center of integration from within the psyche of the adult perpetrator, onto a child. Actual incest kills trust, murders the soul.[10] It splits the mind from the body and flattens self-esteem. Incest is the grandiose use of power to cause powerlessness. Actual incest is the turning of a child person into a victimized *thing*. Actual incest is the egotistical sacrifice of a child's safety, dignity, boundaries, and integrity. With actual incest, a terrifyingly destructive inflation of power, knowledge, and sensuality is forced on children. Incest is the intrusive violation of another human soul in the most tender period of its development. It leaves its victim with a paralyzing sense of futility, numbness, emptiness, and a jealously guarded despair.

In this book I will argue that this horrendous pathology is the result of a demise of living mythic-religious symbols in our culture. These apparently no longer resonate in the depths of the psyche so as to provide a vessel for transpersonal integration and wholeness.

More and more, the Western ego personality has become secularized and personalistic. This has allowed an inflated displacement of the psyche's spiritual impulse to wholeness, causing the compulsion of actual incest, and the addictive intensification of romance, drugs, and food in our society.

In his monumental work *The Decline of the West*, Oswald Spengler pointed out that the twelfth century was the epoch of "the great I."[11] In artistic technique, in romance, and in morality, that period of history witnessed an enormous eruption of *personal* self-consciousness.

From the twelfth century one can trace the first rudimentary impulses to linear perspective in drawing, which subsequently enabled the artist to fashion a unique view of the natural world as if seen through the vision of a single observer. In this same period a new courtly literature focused upon the birth of romantic love in the discriminating heart of a particular human being as he gazed, enraptured, upon the singular features of his lady-love. And it was in this same century that there arose in the collective religious psyche a rapidly building tension between the claims of Christ and the Devil for possession of each human soul.

The Gothic age was increasingly preoccupied with the mounting difficulty of preserving one's own free will to choose good over evil. These two opposite forces were experienced inwardly through the individual's own subjective impulses. The tension between good and evil was not new to the twelfth century, but it became increasingly personalized. Men and women felt themselves to be influenced by a cross-current of malevolent and beneficent forces. After a dark age governed by divine fate, one had now to be constantly on one's guard, lest one fall inescapably into the grip of evil power, thereby relinquishing forever any hope of heaven.

It was in this period that religious sensibilities became increasingly preoccupied with contrition. The Church required that each Christian, in order to be relieved from the burden of his or her own particular sins, must periodically attend a private confession in the sacrament of penance. The priest who heard such a confession and pronounced absolution from God held the delegated power of the keys to heaven and hell from his bishop. This episcopal authority in turn received his own license, it was believed, through the Roman pope from Christ himself.

Whereas in earlier days the practice of Christianity emphasized the incorporation of the individual into the organic spiritual community of the Church, which was conceived to be Christ's mystical body on earth, by the twelfth century it had increasingly become the lonely and sometimes quite alienated struggle of the solitary person to free himself from victimization by sin, with, of course, the indispensable aid of Mother Church's seven sacraments.

It was in just such an artistic, psychological, and spiritual climate that the first stirrings of a truly individual human experience were being felt in Western civilization. Something very new and entirely unique in the history of all human life was afoot, and we today are the inheritors of the boons and the fearsome pitfalls of this nascent development.

Spengler has suggested that the practice of private religious confession arising in the Middle Ages was indeed the beginning of our modern sense of individual biography. "To make one's confession is not to avow an act but to lay before the Judge the inner history of that act," he wrote.[12]

The key dilemma that this book addresses is the grave danger, but also the supreme value, of individual development in relation to the depths of the unconscious psyche when, in our postmodern period, increasing numbers of people may no longer live simply by following the dictates of external authority and rigid tradition.

Rather, they must begin really to acknowledge and reflect upon the spiritual authority and path toward wholeness and truth that lie within the hinterland of the soul.

As we begin this exploration of ourselves through *Gregorius*, it is extremely important to keep in mind that none of it should be taken literally or concretely. None of the characters that appear in the tale are ourselves in the simplest sense of the word. They are each forces or aspects of our lives. We ought not to identify directly or exclusively with any of them. We might think of the different characters and situations as symbols of the basic energy systems that function at deeper levels within the human psyche.

Our tale depicts for us not actual outer physical events, but the drama of inner psychological events in the guise of outer physical events. This legend is contained within the soul of the person of European heritage and will increasingly come to reside in those people who are touched and influenced by a European spirit that values the unfolding life of the self-responsible individual.

ONE

GOD'S OWN MAN

OUR story opens many, many years ago in Rome. The entire
population of citizens is in an uproar because the pope has just
died. The Holy Father is barely in his grave when contending
factions are already striving with one another to choose his
successor. Every leading citizen of the city is trying to get one of
his own relatives elected to the throne so that he too can enjoy the
power and the profit of this highest office. The bickering and
competition reach such a fever pitch that jealousy and greed
prevent these Romans from conceding the choice to any one of
the candidates.

Eventually the wisest among the Romans finally realize that
the situation has become intolerable. They counsel a mor-
atorium, advising their fellow Romans to devote themselves earnestly to prayer and almsgiving while waiting patiently for a
message from the Lord himself. From then on, everyone awaits a

sign from God indicating the right man for the throne of Saint Peter.

Before long, something miraculous happens. One evening, as two wise and devout Romans are engaged in prayer, each in his own house, they hear an identical message from God. A decision has been made from on high. The chosen person is a man named Gregory. He is not an official candidate at all! He is not even a Roman citizen, but is described as a solitary hermit who has been chained for seventeen years on a wild and lonely rock in the sea, somewhere off the coast of Aquitaine. The recipients of this divine revelation are instructed to announce the message and then go search for this man and bring him back to Rome as the new pope.

After the two worthy gentlemen confirm their simultaneous revelations, they announce this divine message to the citizens at large. Then they make preparations to depart on their long journey in search of the newly elect of God, the man called Gregory.

Like these zealous Romans, we all yearn to move forward in our lives, to make progress and achieve success in the world. Such strivings are relatively legitimate as far as our outer life is concerned. But there is indeed another level, that of inner development. It follows different laws and requires that we clearly focus on those goals and objectives that are needed for the wholeness and completeness of our individual selves.

In a sense, we live with a foot in two different camps. One is the arena of the wider collective environment, which we increasingly enter and assimilate as we grow from youth to maturity. Here, our goal is to carve out a place for ourselves in society. This is where we "earn our spurs" and achieve something of value by entering a job or profession and making our mark in the world. It is also the place where we attempt to establish and maintain lasting personal relationships, enter into an intimate connection with a partner, and raise children in such a manner that they can make a viable place for themselves in the community.

But all the while there is another dimension of living that is increasingly ignored as we venture out into an exploration of the world and take our place in the surrounding culture. It is a kind of inner home base, which we vaguely recollect from childhood and to which we frequently return in our meandering day fantasies and in our night dreams—but in a rather subliminal and mostly unconscious way.

We all, sooner or later, begin to feel the call of this inner realm, which constantly attempts to move us by its fearful and attractive images. These come to us through fantasy and dream, in association with certain very compelling thoughts and moods, which have a way of gaining power over us.

The goal of the interior Self is to produce a whole and integrated state of being that is not totally dependent upon the values, strategies, and limitations of outer collective life. Over the long course of individual experience, one may notice the effect of a central guidance system that seems to possess an age-old wisdom regarding the human potential for living. It is as if the psyche contains the accumulated experience of the entire human race, derived from the history of our evolution from millions of years ago. This is present in much the same manner in which our biology preserves the traces of its previous development in its genetic codes. As life progresses, we encounter a divided allegiance between the inner need to grow and develop according to our inherent nature, on the one hand, and our allegiance to the standardized forms of our culture on the other. However, in our society, there is a vast range in degree of how conscious any particular person is of this split in allegiances.

In our tale, the Roman citizens who strive for power and profit are motivated by the collective need for eminence and prestige, and by the praise that others will surely give them if they are "well connected." These people are oblivious to any deeper motive beyond this striving for popular distinction.

As we make our way in the world, it is vitally important that we not confuse these two different levels of consideration. We have an inner life and an outer life. They are both important and are certainly related, but they are not the same thing. Jesus' saying "Render unto Caesar the things that are Caesar's, and unto God the things that are God's,"[1] is a traditional formulation of this need to separate certain basic levels in our psychological awareness.

We often speak of "personality" as the sum of all the distinctive traits of a person's character that can be evaluated by others in the world. In the popular sense, the personality is the outer aspect of our psychological reality, which communicates something recognizable to the surrounding society. Jung used the term *persona* to indicate the outer side of our psychological makeup. This persona, or mask, gives us our external, more collective identity in the world. Many of our willful ambitions for success are based upon a desire to attain an attractive persona in society by "getting ahead" and, like the Romans in our tale, attempting to achieve recognition in the world.

But ever since ancient times, there has been a well-recognized compensation to such persona-oriented schemes for measuring and attaining success. Contrasted with such outer collective means was the notion of a "calling" or "vocation." *Vocation* literally means to be "called" in the sense of actually being addressed by a voice. This is the summons from the inner realm that leads the individual away from reliance upon the outer status-oriented schemes for success toward a deeper and more individual goal of wholeness and the integrity of the Self.

Our persona-mask gives us the means to *feign* individuality, whereas in reality we are merely playing a standard role in a highly collective drama.[2] This role has been instilled in us through our upbringing and exterior education, which is really an indoctrination. The deeper individuation is a development from *within*. It has a transpersonal source within the psyche that is beyond ego consciousness.

Jung uses the term *individual* not to suggest personalistic eccentricity but according to its real sense, which means a unique instance of the "undividable," the whole, or the complete. An "individual" is unique according to mass-minded culture, but universal according to human nature itself.

In our tale, the wise and devout gentlemen hear the voice of God telling them of the man Gregory, who has been living all alone on a rock in the wilderness. This is an important clue concerning the integrity of our inner lives. The man alone in the wilderness is that part of ourselves which remains unrecognized by our collective ambition for success.

The self we might live—the real self—is the forbidden self. Our ambitions are far more collective than we think. In the context of these strivings for competence and success, our uniquely real selves are often marginalized. In the collectively programmed environment of the well-adjusted and successful person, it is a high crime to live one's genuine life in depth. A role must be successfully played, or we lose face. In a climate of collective conformity, an authentic man or woman is often considered to be a nobody. Such a prejudicial program is not only all around us in our society; we internalize it and callously reinforce it inside our very beings. We are embarrassed about the unconventional outsider in the deep recesses of our souls. But this does not prevent our implicit integrity from gnawing at us. We long to meet this side of ourselves, but we generally seek it in a projected and sentimentalized form. Suitably clothed and equipped by L. L. Bean, Eastern Mountain Sports, and Banana Republic, we roam the countryside, or the backyard, in search of our forbidden authenticity.

Somewhere deep within, we all have a hermit who lives alone in the wilderness outside of our adjustment to the surrounding culture. This has nothing to do with external alienation or lack of friends or companionship. The inner aloneness is the state of the personality when it lives on the basis of its own resources, struggling as consciously as possible to acknowledge and integrate its conflicting impulses, and not simply according to the conventional status requirements or unwitting conformities of the herd. This inner solitary figure is our identity *behind* the mask. It is that individual who may indeed play a role in the world, but it is not the role itself. Gregory symbolizes our capacity for introversion. It is this disposition that our two devout Romans go off to seek.

The English word *alone* actually means "all one." The more we focus on our inner aloneness and give consideration to its legitimate needs, the more complete, accurate, and objective our perceptions and judgments will be, and the more we will be able to enter into healthy, intimate, and constructive relationships with other people. The more we are "all one" on the inside, the greater will be our solidarity with all our fellow human beings on the outside.

As with the medieval Romans in our story, it is becoming increasingly evident today that persons with only a mass consciousness, who live only exteriorly, are unable to take real responsibility for themselves or for others. They possess no individual standpoint for judgment and discrimination. Rather, by their shallow passivity, infantile dependency, emotional drivenness, and vulnerability to peer pressure, they may lead us all to the brink of disaster, under the tutelage of various totalitarian regimes, of which they are ultimately the creators. Jung has told us that religion is a counterbalance to mass-mindedness:

> It builds up a reserve, as it were, against the obvious and inevitable force of circumstances to which everyone is exposed who lives only in the outer world and has no other ground under his feet except the pavement. . . . Religion, however, teaches another authority opposed to that of the "world." The doctrine of the individual's dependency upon God makes just as high a claim upon him as the world does.[3]

For a person who has not shrunk from the challenges and obligations of outer life, an enormous amount of freedom and vibrant energy can be released when he or she spends at least a little time "hiding out" from the affairs of outer existence. On one level, at least, we really don't belong to the world, but rather to our inner selves. It is generally invigorating to come home to roost once in a while and simply be who we are inside of ourselves, for better or worse.

It is said that the chosen one, Gregory, has been living alone on a rock for seventeen years. A large rock suggests an underlying reality or basic foundation that lies below our ephemeral worldly experience. Gregory is not our ordinary ego consciousness, but an inner figure. Gregory is our forbidden self.

This "Gregory" part of us has no reputation to defend, no dutiful obligations to perform, no self-esteem to protect or enhance, and no need to prove self-worth by acquiring power or position. He has no role to play. Gregory is beyond moral self-respect. If we are able to connect with our inner Gregory, the yoke of incessant collective striving is lifted from our tired psychological shoulders, so that we might regain our independent human stature and dignity with peace of mind and a deeper appreciation of ourselves and a calmer acceptance of life.

There is an old Japanese Zen saying that gives us the same sense of inner wisdom: "There is no place to which we must go, and there is no thing that we have to do." Another saying, from the ancient Hindu Upanishads, is "While remaining still, we overtake those who are running."

The loss of such a centeredness in our modern existence is no doubt what Yeats had in mind when he wrote in "The Second Coming":

> Turning and turning in the widening gyre
> The falcon cannot hear the falconer;
> Things fall apart; the center cannot hold;
> Mere anarchy is loosed upon the world.[4]

It is important not to take the Gregory tale or its interpretation literally. Finding and holding such a center is no easy task. Actually going and sitting on a desolate rock somewhere will hardly get anyone elected pope in the literal and concrete world. Just sitting and doing nothing as a whole program of life is not a possible or even healthy alternative for most Western people today. We all have a busy outer existence that needs to be lived and that itself gives us a valuable anchoring in a certain context of reality.

Our outer life and our ego consciousness are like a boat that keeps us afloat on the great sea of the unconscious. From it we might fish for inner food and make occasional explorations into the depths for self-knowledge and renewal. Because our story is fictional, it speaks a metaphoric language about *inner* things. If we rush ahead and naively apply inner laws to outward situations, we will at best make utter fools of ourselves, like Don Quixote, who mistook windmills for giants and heroically charged at them, brandishing his lance.

The object of our search is a new "pope," to resolve our dilemma. One of the most important of the pope's traditional titles is Pontifex Maximus, meaning "Highest Priest." This title, adopted by the early popes, was originally held by the Roman emperors of pagan antiquity, signifying that they were the highest members of the Roman guild of religious functionaries. *Pontifex* literally means "bridge-builder." Therefore, the pope is believed to function symbolically as the connecting link between human nature and God. In traditional Roman Catholic belief, the Holy Father is tantamount to the actual earthly presence of Christ himself as head of the Church. As Christ's direct personal representative, or "vicar," it is he who is ultimately responsible for the authoritative and unerring teaching of the faith.

Psychologically, our "pope aspect" is an inner aspect of the personality that bridges the gap between our ordinary ego consciousness and the deeper realm of archetypal wisdom in the collective unconscious. This is the Wise Old Man archetype, the ultimate source of truth, power, and meaning in our lives. He connects us to what we might call the "architectural plans" of our universal human nature. Jung likened this complex of basic psychological structures to the comparative anatomy of the physical body, which takes a unique form in every individual, but which is universally human in its general features.

Our pope aspect is the deep *authority* that exists in our inner selves. It is he who makes it possible for us to know and follow the real truth of our own lives, regardless of what is pressing or fashionable in the surrounding culture. This inner figure is able to take a stand on solid ground within our souls. It is important to realize that our pope aspect is not simply our ego, nor is it any whimsical impulse, or merely the internalization of social mores, collective consensus, or conventional belief. It is no superego. It is more like a very profound and independent inner conscience that is far wiser than "I" could ever be. Our pope aspect is an original inner source of authentic truth. In no sense is it a body of knowledge or understandings imparted to us by our parents or by our social upbringing. This does not come to us automatically, nor are we taught much about it in school. We must go in search of it.

Peter, the chief apostle, who tradition says was the first pope, had the rock as his chief symbol. "Upon this rock I shall build my church,"[5] says Jesus in the Gospel narrative. Also, his name, Peter, was commonly associated to the Greek and Latin word for rock, *petra*.

As a great rock is nearly everlasting and because it possesses such mass, it represents a stable and completely earthbound basis for practical reality. Any wisdom, guidance, or program for fathoming life must rest upon such a secure foundation in ordinary existence. A great truth is generally convincing and "rings true" because, although it inspires and uplifts us, giving us a vision of things beyond the mundane, it is nonetheless convincing on a practical level. It makes obvious good sense and anchors us securely in reality. Theodore Roosevelt understood a bit of this when he advised, "Keep your eyes on the stars and your feet on the ground!"

In the old biblical story, the young patriarch-to-be, Jacob, stopped one evening on his travels and lay down to sleep, using a stone for a pillow. In the night he dreamed of a ladder standing on the ground with its top reaching to heaven. There were angels of God going up the ladder and coming down. Then God appeared, standing over him, and spoke about Jacob's destiny and the future of his people. When Jacob awakened and remembered the events of his dream, he set up the stone as a monument, and called the place Beth-el, or "House of God."[6]

Like the lone man Gregory in our tale, Jacob knew where to put his head! Both stories are telling us that if we orient our minds to a simple and basic reality, right down on the ground, so to speak, and do this on our solitary inner journey through life, then we shall experience the union and interrelationship between the highest and lowest things. It will be as if heaven and earth did indeed come together. And this will be the occasion for a vocation, or calling, to follow the course of our own unique lives.

In the end, neither Gregory nor Jacob tried to climb the ladder of success and prominence to the ultimate station in life. They remained alone and down low. From this basic level, devoid of prestige, they were raised to preeminence among their people.

TWO

INCEST

AS our two Roman gentlemen begin their long search for God's chosen one, let us go back about fifty years in time to the period about one generation before the birth of the man named Gregory.

In the south of France, the Duke of Aquitaine and his consort have just had boy and girl twins, the most ravishingly beautiful children the world has ever seen. Scarcely has the mother been delivered of her babies than she dies in childbed. The infants survive, healthy and well cared for.

Just ten years later, the duke himself lies mortally ill. He laments the fact that he has made no provision for his daughter's eventual marriage. After witnessing his vassals' oaths of fealty to his son and heir, the duke reminds the boy to care for his sister, and then he dies.

As the twins grow up, they are inseparable. The brother makes every effort to love and protect his sister, and always tries to please her. She returns her brother's love with deep appreciation and affection. The two enjoy an idyllic life together, attended by an admiring household and court.

But the Devil envies the great respect and high regard that are constantly paid these aristocratic children. He formulates a malevolent plan to rob them of their high honor and esteem, and turn their great joy into sorrow.

The Devil uses the sister's rare beauty to incite lust in the brother. Then the Evil One adds an overbearing arrogance to the boy's character, which, combined with the young duke's still childish disposition, leads the brother to think about actually having carnal sex with his sister.

One night, while the sister is fast asleep, the boy slips stealthily into her bed and takes her by surprise. His ardent caresses awaken her. As he wrestles with her, she is on the verge of screaming for help when she realizes that if someone were to discover them, they would both suffer the loss of all their honor and bright fame. This thought keeps her from crying out.

The girl struggles, but her brother finally overpowers her and has his way. In subsequent weeks the twins innocently enjoy their newly found pleasure. But the day arrives when the sister discovers that she is pregnant. Then all their joy is turned to pain.

Orphaned children commit incest! What is the meaning of this shocking revelation? Psychologically, the aristocratic parents of the twins in our tale represent a version of the Self. As Jung has pointed out, the chief symbol of the Self in folklore and religious literature the world over is the archetype of the sacred marriage, which is generally represented by the conjugal union of an aristocratic or cosmic pair. These may include a sacred king and queen, a prehistoric or mythic father and mother, god and goddess, heaven and earth, the concept of spirit and nature united, or a more abstract symbolic image like the *yin* and *yang* of Chinese Taoist philosophy.

Judaism gave expression to this sacred marriage in the covenanted union of God with Israel, and in the earthbound and heaven-bound conjunction of two triangles forming the Star of David. Christians visualized the nuptial union of the Holy Spirit of God with the Virgin Mary, Christ the Bridegroom and his Bride the Church, or the mystical marriage of the soul with God.

In Jungian psychology, the Self is the psychological center of wholeness and completeness. It represents the union of all opposites and conflicts within the psyche, bringing peace, unity, and fulfillment to the soul. The Self is synonymous with the individual's image of God as it is actually experienced psychologically.

In our tale, a transpersonal image, that of the archetypally united masculine and feminine principles, has disappeared from consciousness with the death of the duke and his consort. The children are left without any traditional version or exemplification of this image, against which they can measure the development of their own lives as conscious human beings. They, like us, are psychospiritual orphans.

As orphans, the twins are deprived of witnessing objectively this archetypal incestuous mystery of wholeness and psychic union, which the parents would have otherwise portrayed to them.

It may seem absurd to suggest that the archetypal marriage of parents is "incestuous." To understand this, one must realize that children experience their parents in a vastly different way than the actual parents regard their own conjugal relationship. Children cannot imagine that their parents enjoy a relation markedly different from the one that they, as children, have with each other and with the parents. From the children's perspective, all relations within the family are psychologically consanguineous.

Children cannot imagine or tolerate the idea that at one time their parents were not intimate participants in the same nuclear family, that originally they were perfect strangers to each other. Children cannot imagine that their parents are like anything other than brother and sister to each other. The exclusive erotic intimacy that the parents enjoy, and from which the children are excluded, is an intensely provocative mystery to them. This is precisely the reason why teenage and even adult children have great trouble imagining their parents engaging in sexual intercourse. The whole thing is taboo to the children—unthinkable, repulsive, even disgusting. It is forbidden. It is incestuous. It is divine!

The masculine and feminine halves of the Self form an "incestuous" union because these figures symbolize the union of the psyche with itself, which produces the integration of *one* interior reality—the wholeness of the entire personality. In outer life the solidarity of the parents' mutual love and devotion serves as a living and protecting symbol of the Self for their children. In infancy, the parents are indeed the cosmic reality within which the children must live in trust.

In our tale, the symbolic parents who portray the incestuous union of opposites are now dead. The archetypal energy still exists, but it is now in the unconscious and can no longer be experienced by projection onto the actual parents. In other words, the parents are no longer living objective symbols of the Self in consciousness for the children. Under these circumstances what happens to the sacred marriage archetype? What will fill in the vacancy in consciousness left by the dead parents? This is where a grave problem, a really tragic problem, arises for the twins—and for us modern folk.

Our authoritative God-image has died. It has gone unconscious. We no longer appreciate what masculinity and femininity are. We have no idea of how they ought properly to be related to each other. We have little understanding of the nature and functioning of parenting, and less of how parents themselves ought to behave, or precisely how they should relate to each other or to their children. In contemporary society many parents are themselves emotionally children. They struggle with their own offspring for power and influence within the family, and often use their children to satisfy their own neurotic needs. The archetype of the sacred marriage, which should inform all this, seems nowhere in our world to be held up before us as a cogent symbol in our cultural awareness.

What seems obvious is that the twins take on this archetypal and divine role themselves. They naively and unconsciously identify with the divine marriage archetype and, like the gods and goddesses of old, enter into an incestuous relationship. They come to signify to others and to each other the mystery of divine life. From the twins' personal level as ordinary human beings, this assumption of transpersonal significance amounts to grandiosity. This is more and more our contemporary mentality. Our traditional image for the experience of divine reality has died—it has fallen into the unconscious—so we have presumptuously stepped into this vacuum with our egos. God is really not dead. We ourselves have become gods and goddesses, and woe be to anyone who tries to tell us how to live our lives or what truth we must follow. We know best. We've got all the answers.

Theologically and mythically we still retain a pale exterior skeleton of the old rich informing symbols, in the literatures, arts, and liturgies of Christianity, Judaism, and Islam, for instance. But they rarely work for educated and worldly people in any depth. We chew on the menu repeatedly, but it is exceptional for anyone to digest the meal itself.

This stepping into a transpersonal role way beyond our down-to-earth human capacity, Jung called *inflation*. For the twins, left psychologically unprotected by their parents' death, their childish immaturity was inflated by the intrusive dark and repressed side of the God-image, the "Devil." Their beautiful and idyllic world was shattered, not unlike the loss of Paradise in the biblical episode.

Impersonating gods is very dangerous. Inflation can be devastating. We become inflated whenever we are overpowered by an archetypal force of the psyche. Whenever we fall victim to the subliminal whim of any impulse or emotion, so that we lose the power of conscious consideration and choice, we are inflated. When we indulge our temper or appetite, or when we are simply "beside ourselves," then we are inflated. We are inflated whenever we try to possess another person, control his life or existence, use him to meet our own needs and appetites, or force him to be or do what we want. We are also inflated when we compulsively or unmercifully try to control ourselves. We modern people are inflated most of the time. It is practically the normal way of life in our present-day culture.

Let us pause for a moment and look at the dream of a fifty-year-old California art teacher. In her youth her mother was alcoholic, while her father constantly locked himself up in his artist's studio, where he was both physically and emotionally unavailable. The woman recalls that she never received any praise from her father but that she absolutely "adored" him from afar. The dreamer never witnessed any affection between her parents. She says she was molested on numerous occasions by her older brother and his friend when she was between the ages of eleven and thirteen. At that time she complained to her mother, but nothing effective was done. Here is the woman's dream:

> I am sitting on a curbside. I have a penis. My daughter, Stephanie, is sitting on my lap. I have my arms around her and am making love to her. It is very loving, no sense of shame. "Is it all right?" I whisper in her ear. "Yes, Mommy," she replies, "it's fine." [Though the daughter is twenty years old in real life, she appears in the dream as about thirteen.]

This dream indicates that the woman is not functioning in her own life as a feminine being. Her having a penis means she is identified with her masculinity—with her animus side—and not at all with her femininity. Here the masculinity is superior in authority to the feminine, in the mode of parent to child. They are not equals.

Because the dreamer's parents exhibited no feeling relation in front of the children, probably enjoyed precious little of it between themselves, and were emotionally unavailable, the dreamer has completely identified with her father. She has done this to close the intolerable gap between herself and him. Thus she connects to her own femininity (symbolized by her daughter) in the mode of father-daughter incest.

To overcome the distancing of her father from her, she has simply become like him, psychologically a masculine person. The pronounced sense of love and intimacy in the dream incest is precisely what was missing both between the parents and between the father and the daughter. The dreamer is perilously trying to make over her father's attitude to meet her own needs, but this is distorting her life and depriving her of her feminine standpoint. One suspects that in real life, the dreamer "fathers" her daughter rather than mothering her.

Apparently the archetypal masculine principle was neither exhibited nor mediated to the family by the father. So it inflates out of the unconscious and causes the incestuous tendency in the brother at the low level of physical molestation. The patriarchal inflation enters the dreamer's psyche by seizing and replacing her feminine ego. She is psychologically now a man, not a woman. As an alcoholic, the dreamer's mother was largely incapable of portraying a strong and authentic femininity for her daughter's benefit in her marriage to her artist-husband.

The personal father represents traditional collective consciousness (Freud's "superego"). This severely dominates the dreamer's own feminine attitude, causing her to be overly rigid, structured, and "safe" in all her dealings in life. She must be careful always to do the "right" thing. Spontaneity is difficult for her, and impulsive or random changes in the patterns of her life create anxiety and mistrust.

The daughter, Stephanie, is the dreamer's virginal feminine quality. It ought properly to be open to the impulse of the transpersonal Spirit, so that a "virgin birth" of creative and spontaneous life could ensue. But this possibility is thwarted by an intrusion of the collective-mindedness of the father tradition, to which the dreamer has aligned herself. The dreamer has made a "god" out of her father and is inflatedly identified with him.

Notice that the action happens on the street curb. Such a location generally signifies the place of lowest and most common value, completely public with no privacy or individuality. This suggests that for the dreamer, femininity is utterly pedestrian and not at all special. She "learned" this from her father's oblivious attitude toward her. The curb also suggests restraint and control. Her creative femininity is "curbed" by her father complex.

In real life the dreamer presents a persona of genteel femininity. She is well-mannered, gracious, correct in her demeanor, though overly efficient, organized, controlled, and disciplined. But underneath, in the unconscious psyche, the dream shows her as a man, intrusively violating the rich feminine possibilities of living that would bring her human nature some peace and the joy of instinctive freedom.

For us, inflation is particularly evident in the widespread phenomenon called "loss of self-esteem." When we feel like the worst person, at the very bottom of the totem pole, totally unsuccessful, swimming in inferiority, riddled with unworthiness, then we are inflated. This is because we are constantly measuring our value and capability against a grandiose but quite unconscious scale of completely overblown expectations, and so we feel inferior. When we feel that much like a miserable worm, we would do well to get tough and say to ourselves, "What earthly right do I have to feel so colossally terrible? I am only human. I am not allowed to feel *that* bad. Only a god would have that right!"

In general, inflation means that the individual human ego has regressed to a childish state of unconscious grandiosity, overstepped its legitimate human limitations, and is "playing God." It has gotten swallowed up by an archetype. People who have climbed up into inflation will never listen to reason, other people's cautionary advice, or practical sense. They know best automatically. When we are inflated, we can never accept ourselves as simple, ordinary, down-to-earth human beings.

In our tale, the brother and sister have been abandoned by their parents' death. Whenever actual parents are physically or emotionally absent from their children—when they are unable or unwilling to function responsibly as adult parents—an inflated sense of importance and a grandiose assumption of responsibility arise in the children. Such children end up behaving as if they were little gods, generally by succumbing to an intense anxiety whenever they cannot control the world around them in prodigious fashion, or by unmercifully manipulating others as a way of gaining security and sufficient personal recognition. The literature of Alcoholics Anonymous and its "Adult Children of Alcoholics" (ACOA) program is filled with descriptions of such problems. It is worthwhile reading for alcoholics and non-alcoholics alike for the insights it gives into this pervasive modern difficulty. [1]

Such unwitting grandiosity is running rampant in our society today. It is behind the characteristic narcissism evidenced by our contemporary culture. We increasingly demand bigger houses, more electronic conveniences and expensive adult "toys," luxurious vacations far from home, and grandiose "images" to describe our lifestyles. I recently drove past a new condominium development in the Midwest where an enormous sign on the gaudily decorated gate piers advertised, "Versailles Estates." People who take such pompous grandiosity seriously are just asking for the terror and pain of psychological revolution.

Why are the royal twins of our tale lovers? The image of incest is an ancient and powerful one. Of our inner partners, the anima is the inner "mother-sister-daughter" of a man. The animus is the inner "father-brother-son" of a woman. They are of the "same blood" because they are of the same person—ourselves.

In the divine realm, incest abounds. Zeus and Hera were husband and wife but also brother and sister. The Egyptian god Osiris and his consort goddess Isis were brother and sister. These divine siblings mated while still fetuses in their own mother's womb to produce Horus, the sun god. Horus was born at the same time as his parents! The great Germanic hero Siegfried was the offspring of a brother-sister union between Sigmund and Siglinde. In Nordic myth the God Frey, dispenser of peace and prosperity, was the product of brother-sister incest, and he himself was married to his own sister Freia, goddess of love and beauty. In the biblical tale of Adam and Eve, it is told that Eve was taken from Adam's side while he was in a deep sleep.[2] Our mythical first parents therefore formed an incestuous marriage, having originally been of the very same blood. And the Hebrew Sarah conceived a son, Isaac, by her half brother Abraham.[3]

In late medieval alchemy—which was really more concerned with the workings of the inner imagination than with actual physical chemistry as we now know it—an important stage of transformation in the process of making gold (which symbolized luminous consciousness) was represented by the copulation of a king and queen who were brother and sister. This image appears in a series of woodcuts illustrating an alchemical text, the *Rosarium Philosophorum* (1550). In an illustration preceding by three stages that of the incestuous coitus, the king and queen are depicted with their left hands joined.[4] This "sinister" (meaning "left" in Latin) marriage is the archetypal interior union, not the "dexter" (meaning "right") union based upon projection onto outer physical, human, personal, and sociological events. It is "sinister" because it runs counter to the morally approved requirement of the social marriage contract in the patriarchal world. Such a "left-handed" union is a marriage according to nature, impulse, and spontaneous love inwardly directed, guided neither by society nor moral laws, nor by institutionalized theology, economics, or politics. Such a marriage is strictly a matter of the heart and soul. It is within such a realm that the divine archetypal forces are free to act, regardless of merely human categories or conventional restraints.

If either of the aristocratic twins in our tale had married in the usual way, this would have symbolized the projection of the animus or anima. Psychologically a "husband" symbolizes a projected animus; a "wife," a projected anima. In our tale, this would have been signified by the twins making an erotic bond with someone from outside, someone of "other blood." Interest and psychological energy (libido) would have flowed out into the world as a form of extraversion, which would have led consciousness to new, though illusory, experiences and encounters in the outside world, but, at the same time, increasingly further from the inner Self, the archetypal or spiritual foundation of existence.

But if the twins had followed such projections (if the duke had indeed betrothed his daughter) and if each had attempted to make a bond with someone outside the family on the basis of these projections, psychological incest would merely have been displaced, and therefore dissipated, to the arena of outer relationship, and they would have attempted to mate with the exteriorized image of brother or sister or mother or father, projected in the guise of another actual person.

This inner mating must take place—we have virtually no choice in the matter. It is as irresistible and compelling for us as it is for the twins in our story. The increasing failure of marriages today indicates that we are all performing this kind of vicarious incest with abandon, without the slightest idea of what we are really doing. We call it "passion," "romance," and "falling in love." The failure of conjugal relations and the demise of living religious symbols go hand in hand. They are merely two sides of the very same coin. Our romantic encounters that are so "electric" are simply displacements of the dynamic God-image from the interior realm of the soul to an interpersonal erotic event. This is really a form of idolatry.

A direct relation to the anima/animus gives a man or woman a real basis for his or her own healthy and independent experience of rapture, truth, and security, so that neither will need to neurotically depend upon or manipulate his or her mate. In this way both are liberated from compulsive passion and unrealistic romantic fantasy, and are enabled to love and acknowledge each other powerfully and genuinely. It is as if the archetype of the sacred marriage lives within each independent human personality. This is symbolic incest.

A happily married man once dreamt the following:

My wife, Abigail, and I are attending Richard Wagner's opera *Parsifal*. The last act begins where the Knights of the Grail and King gather around the table. Suddenly Abigail moves to another seat two rows ahead, leaving a vacant seat between us. I am instantly aware that everything on the stage is now "real" and not an act. The Grail appears with a red glow of majestic power and holiness. When the King, who seems also to be a priest, takes the cup in his hands and raises it to his lips, three events take place simultaneously: the King's lips touch the rim of the cup; an image appears in the air above the cup of two young Romeo and Juliet—type lovers kissing; and Abigail reaches back and I reach forward, and our fingertips touch ever so lightly. Then everything is filled with a glorious and ecstatic feeling of love and fulfillment. It is as if the heart and soul of life had been united and touched our beings to the core!

In this dream it is apparent that the archetypal level of the sacred marriage occurs on the stage represented by the King (the masculine principle) drinking from the Grail cup (the feminine principle represented by a vessel) as well as by the two young lovers kissing. The dreamer and his wife are clearly differentiated from each other and from the level of sacred and erotic action taking place on the stage. Their lives "touch" with a powerful feeling of completion.

This mysterious union at the erotic and sacred levels does not take place primarily between this man and his wife, but beyond them, on the stage. The married couple in the audience watch this and experience it indirectly as observers, not as the principal players. They themselves are not god and goddess or Romeo and Juliet, but these archetypal alliances grace their lives. The dreamer feels the energy of the dramatic union, but he is not identified with it.

In love relations today, instead of remaining ordinary human beings and finding a symbolic-mythic way to honor objectively the incestuous nuptials of god and goddess as archetypal and transpersonal realities, we have abandoned our merely human identity and have naively but presumptuously wandered into the Divine Bridal Chamber. We do this because we are seduced by the ecstasy of it. It feels so good. This is a typical symptom of inflation.

As far as our tale is concerned, it appears that a movement toward wholeness and individual consciousness is beginning to occur, but that it has been short-circuited through an inflation by the dark and erotic side of the God-image. These beautiful aristocratic children seem to have no standpoint in consciousness for judgment or criticism vis-à-vis this devilish impulse.

In all the cultures of the world there has existed a strong taboo against actual incest between closely related individuals of the same family or certain members of the same clan. But at the same time, incest has often been a prerogative and a requirement of both gods and goddesses, and of the various royal figures who have served as their incarnations on earth.

The fact that mythic-royal-divine persons were permitted to engage in incest, but not the common, ordinary person, signifies that incest is properly an aspect of the inner symbolic-archetypal dimension of the psyche, and that the ordinary human ego, the "I," must stay absolutely clear of it, for such an involvement of the ego, or the personal consciousness, would lead to inflation, and on occasion even to a psychopathic acting out of the incest motif in real life.

Because the twins are aristocrats, they do not represent ordinary ego consciousness, but rather archetypal energy states within the psyche. Therefore, the technicality of their incest is not the basic problem. The real problem is that an erotic-creative and power-wielding side of the God archetype has erupted from deeper unconscious levels, where it has been inordinately repressed by the values of Christian civilization, and has contaminated the newly forming image of sacred marriage in the medieval psyche. It is the violent rape of the sister by her brother that is the problem. The phallic power of the Devil is the repressed earthy, subterranean fertility side of the divine energy of life. That erupted and took possession of the brother, who forcibly possessed his sister. This is the deeper source and origin of what we today call sexual abuse. Such behavior is typical of a one-sidedly patriarchal disposition.

Literal involvement in incest has always been and is still considered one of the most hideous, destructive, and repulsive crimes imaginable. This is a result of the effect of the age-old incest taboo on our sensibilities. Psychologically there are two perfectly justifiable purposes for this taboo. One is an outer or extraverted reason, the other an inner or introverted one.

The introverted purpose of the taboo is to block outward expression of a certain portion of love and sexuality and redirect it back toward its source in the unconscious, in order to produce an interior awareness of transpersonal reality, formed by an inverted reflection of psychic energy back upon itself. This liberates us from the overpowering enthrallment of Mother Nature's instinct and awakens our human capacity for lucid and objective intelligence.

The extraverted, social-psychological purpose of the incest taboo is to protect us all from the devastating power of one another's inner god or goddess. We shun incest outwardly to properly discriminate the human-personal from the divine-archetypal, in such a way that we may love and respect, rather than grandiosely use and dominate, each other. The incest taboo is a kind of armor we wear to protect ourselves from the divine energy in another person, especially our parents, siblings, children, or secondarily from those with whom we may be tempted to fall passionately in love.

Concrete incest is so destructive—not so much because of biological inversion as because it results when one person seizes authoritative sexual dominance as if he or she possessed a divine prerogative. It is the sexual and psychospiritual traumatization of a child or sibling by the depreciated and repressed dark side of the sacred marriage archetype in the inflated person. It is the illicit drawing of a simple mortal into the divine field of high energy. This is why both the adult abuser and even more the child victim often appear to be so unwitting and helpless under the pressure of the compulsion. This disaster also occurs indirectly when unrelated people fall head-over-heels "in love." It is as if both have fallen under the crude power of the dark side of God, masked in apparently human form.

We have failed miserably to deal with this archetypal incest phenomenon in our European-oriented religious culture. It has simply entered by the "back door" of actual incest between parents and children and between siblings, and indirectly in the overly intensified romantic love that destabilizes our families and traumatizes our very hearts.

The fact that incest as a sociopathic phenomenon is being recognized and treated more and more widely today indicates our need to appreciate the importance of this phenomenon on an inner symbolic, as well as on a literal, level of understanding.

Jung felt that the incest taboo is a basic archetypal component of the human personality and that it is one expression of the archetypal power of Spirit. Spirit is that impulse in the psyche that is capable of opposing the unconscious surge of instinct, in order to transform nature into a conscious human experience. The social-symbolic phenomenon resulting from this transformation we know as creative culture.

Jung believed that there is in the human psyche an inherent inhibition against incest with close relatives that serves a definite psychological purpose. This spiritual purpose is to produce a consciousness of an inner erotic image, the anima or animus, which is released by the psychic energy that has been blocked from outward expression, and is reflected back, like light that strikes a mirror. Here within the depths of the psyche the "incest" functions in a very different way, and in a different light.

The regression (literally "going back") and containment of this psychic energy serve to form fantasy and dream images that are not fused to the ego nor thrust upon the outer world through projection. This is precisely the deeper purpose of the age-old ideals of chastity and celibacy the world over. Here outward expression of unrestrained sexuality is curtailed in order to produce a heightened and protected awareness of erotic energy inwardly.

Incest is a double-edged razor. It is frequently the case that what is hideous, abnormal, deranged, destructive, and criminal, when expressed in the outer concrete world, may be utterly beautiful, creative, sane, and sacred when experienced within the soul and acknowledged consciously. This may be the reason why certain old religious terms often carried a grossly ambivalent meaning. For instance, the Latin word *sacer*, which means "sacred," "holy," or "consecrated," can just as well mean "accursed," "devoted to destruction," or "horrible." Incest may bring wholeness and health, or illness and destruction, depending upon where and how it is functioning. It is "horrible" when it functions *between* people and "sacred" when it functions *within* people.

This introverting or "doubling back" of psychic energy is what produces a phenomenal awareness of the archetypal or divine world. Such an interior "incest" gives us our knowledge and experience of transpersonal reality, the royal kingdom that lies within us all. Today, depth psychologists call this "consciousness."

We are committing interior incest, the good kind, when we meditate, engage in contemplative prayer, participate in the symbolic liturgy, pay attention to our dreams, and seriously follow and study the workings of our imagination. Inner incest takes place when we take a serious inventory of our moral assets and liabilities as human beings, when we dialogue with ourselves concerning our ambivalences and inner conflicts, and when we refuse to contaminate the surrounding world with our projected fantasies and prejudices. This kind of incest is the royal road to the deepest human experience and understanding of life.

In our story, the incest was brought about by the Devil. The Devil envied the twins' idyllic existence and the great adulation and respect paid to them, so he began to make trouble. Archetypally, the Devil is the dark and shadowy side of our God-image. Since the end of classical antiquity, when patriarchal Christian ideals became increasingly dominant in Europe, the natural and impulsive side of the human personality became more and more suspect. Accordingly, the noble ideals of goodness and purity could not accommodate the more instinctive, aggressive, and erotic aspects of experience. So these darker layers, associated with seduction, lust, and fertility, were repressed or devalued. Europe ended up with a relatively good, clean, kind, and sexually innocuous Christ, continually shadowed by the Devil, who increasingly expressed the crudest forms of unbridled pride, ambition, and concupiscence. The wholeness of existence was split apart, and the dark half was condemned out of hand. Christians were continually exhorted to strive for moral perfection and stifle their devilish impulses.

Since the late Middle Ages, the Devil has generally been depicted with a hairy, animal-like body, the horns of a bull, and the cloven hooves of a goat. In the ancient world of pre-Christian antiquity, both these animals were commonly viewed as paragons of lust and concupiscence, but also as gods of fertility. There was nothing evil about them. They represented simply the earthy facts of life. Pan was the ithyphallic (literally "having the penis erect") goat god of the rustic woodland, who played the spiritual harmonies of nature's enchantment on his pipe. Poseidon, the old Greek god, was the divine "bull of the sea." The three-pronged spear or "trident," carried by the Devil, belonged originally to Poseidon.

Since this instinctive and erotic side of mankind's spirituality could find no place in the religious symbolism of Christian culture as a positive or legitimate expression of life's energies, it was banished to the unconscious regions. From there it has constantly threatened to erupt at a moment's notice—and now calls to us for integration. Consequently, it is the darker aspect of the archetype of God by which we are most often seized compulsively, in our fantasies and in our behavior. It is so often in our instinctive appetites that we suffer the addictive compulsions that destroy our well-being and our peace.

Today, our culture's fascination with primitive violence and sex is evidence for this. The crudely explicit scenes of pornographic movies are the dark and repressed side of our worship of God. To the degree that pornography is exciting, titillating, and enervating, it is a displaced and distorted form of religious experience, a primitive and low-level version of the divine marriage of the god and the goddess. We are fascinated by the enchantment of the porno queen in wild gymnastic union with her stud. She functions as our modern priestess of ecstasy.

A man who was addicted to watching pornographic movies once dreamt that he found himself on the top floor of a building. He was dizzy from the height and frightened. Women below shouted for him to come down to the ground where it would be safe. The dreamer identified the building as the parish hall of his childhood church, in which he had been taught his catechism.

The porn queen is a low-level anima image, and this man's irresistible need to indulge his cruder appetites was the psyche's only way of bringing him down to earth from a far too "spiritual" and perfectionistic attitude toward living, an attitude that was far too "high" to be creative or affirm life in any integrative way. I told this man that people with that high a spirituality would no doubt find their own experience of the Virgin Mary in a brothel, symbolically, of course.

In our own lives, whether we are children or adults, any overpowering impulse or compulsive addiction or fascination is an expression of a devalued and repressed archetype that has seized control of the ego. The three primary fields of such an unconscious seizure are food-drink-drugs, sex, and power. Traditional religious ceremonies and sacraments throughout the world have channeled these instinctive energies into rituals of fasting and communion with the deity, and into symbolic enactments of fertility, regeneration, purification, rebirth, and sacrifice to divine omnipotence. In this way, the archetypal forces of the personality were given a symbolic and therefore conscious expression. They were objectified in a sacred ritual at a holy place set apart for the purpose. To declare something sacred and to enact it in rite and ritual means to make it conscious as an objective presence, thereby liberating it from inflated, egotistical, and compulsive necessity. One must put God "out there" in order to escape from the most grotesque of all tragedies, namely, the monstrous inflation of the ego by identification with the divine.

But today, a credible faith in such symbolic rituals is waning, and we are increasingly vulnerable to the darkest forces of crude instinct. Yeats so perceptively queried in "The Second Coming":

> And what rough beast, its hour come round at last,
> Slouches towards Bethlehem to be born?[5]

The "rough beast" to which Yeats alludes must be the animal-phallic-power side of God, which has been almost completely expunged from both Christian dogma and Christian values for living. That is what erupts in our fascination with pornography and crude violence.

The brother initiated the incest. The Devil went to work on the boy, not the girl. This situation is the opposite of that found in the biblical Garden of Eden episode in which Eve is tempted by the serpent and then persuades Adam to eat the apple.

This situation suggests that the solution to our recent psychological predicament since the Middle Ages lies not in ridding ourselves of the "threat" of the feminine, as mankind had sought to do previously. Then, an objective awareness of the empirical world was just arising, and the developing patriarchal task was to devalue and even negate the feminine realm of the instinctive unconscious psyche, to give a clear and detached mental consciousness and self-discipline a chance to grow, without its being continually swallowed up by the sanguine impulses of the flesh, and by a tendency to live according to childlike fantasy, in a world still psychologically under the spell of a fairy-tale enchantment.

When people neurotically fail to develop beyond such a childish psychology, psychoanalysts say that they are pulled down into unconsciousness by "retrogressive incest." This phenomenon applies to people who have failed to develop a sufficient strength of consciousness and responsibility, and who experience their instincts and the fantasies that proceed from them as seductive allurements, drawing them into enticing daydreams that serve as escapes from reality, bringing an infantile kind of pleasure that is self-centered and sterile, a form of psychological masturbation. Such a purely regressive kind of incest should be carefully discriminated from its opposite, "progressive" or "heroic" incest, which describes a courageous and purposeful symbolic journey into the mother unconscious for the purpose of transformation and rebirth. The product of the latter is self-responsible creativity, including the art of living, rather than infantile pleasure.

Our task today is to get beyond our patriarchal tradition as the mere dead hand of the past and to seek a religious consciousness that is the living stuff of inspiration and creative development. The psychological task of the early patriarchal period was to resist nature and spontaneous fantasy in order to build up a field of self-disciplined moral consciousness. To accomplish this it was necessary to repress and devalue the alluring and captivating presence of the feminine—the unconscious surge of instinctive impulse and dream wisdom—so that a higher rational and coherent image of the world could be founded upon empirical evidence.

The task for people today is to lower this rational awareness once again into the instinctive realm of impulse and feeling in order to reclaim what had been jettisoned into the unconscious.

One important thing we must do today is get in touch with male fertility at an archetypal level, in order to transform it into love and creative innovation in our conscious lives. We need to become the creators of culture and a new awareness, not the custodians of a museum of antiquities and a restrictive past. This must happen in the personalities of both men and women.

Symbolic incest is the inner experience of the conjugal union of god and goddess, the fertility rite of the personality. It is the putting back together of that which has gotten split apart. Symbolic incest means "integration," where the personality turns back and reenters itself, and consciousness sinks down into its sister-mother source in the unconscious psyche in order to transform and reproduce itself anew.

Symbolic incest is primarily a religious phenomenon. The English word *religion* comes from the Latin *religio*, which means to unite or tie back together that which has gotten torn apart or fragmented. It is also the root for the word *ligament*. Religion is thus related to a "holiness" that is a true "wholeness," which can bring a healing connectedness, completeness, and peace to the conflicts of the human psyche.

As our mysterious tale unfolds, the offspring of the incestuous twins will have a crucial role to play in relation to this heavenly country of our hearts and souls. He will personify our own struggle, show us the dangerous pitfalls in our psychological existence, and direct us to the proper realization of our archetypally grounded humanity. He will lead us to God.

THREE

◆

LOVE

SUBLIME OR SINISTER

BEFORE continuing further with the narrative of our story, let us pause and reflect more deeply on what has happened.

One detail, easily overlooked, is of particular importance to the chain of events. The duke neglected to betroth his only daughter. This is evidence of a powerful psychological change that was occurring in the twelfth century. In this patriarchal authoritarian age, women were considered to be the exclusive property of men. When a young woman married, she left the confines of her father's jurisdiction only to submit to the rule of her husband. A woman of the medieval period, even if she was of the nobility, was not considered a complete and independent person in her own right. It was a man's world, fearsome and aggressive. All marriages were arranged by the parents, as early as at birth, generally for political and economic consolidation between great families. Young aristocratic men and women were simply the pawns of great interregional dealings. Love played little if any role in such relationships.

The twin sister was not betrothed before her father died. This means that she was not required to submit to male authority in the exterior world of medieval society. Now we understand better why the mother died as soon as the twins were born. The position and value of the feminine as inferior to the masculine, and as the possession of it, was coming to an end, giving birth to the new. That old order of things had died. The feminine was destined to occupy more than simply the secondary position of "wife."

But since the twins' father died when they were only ten years old, this means that the masculine figure is also being subject to an important change. This stage of the tale hints that a gradual and almost subliminal shift in psychology is just starting in the twelfth century. It would eventually end the old one-sidedly patriarchal order. We are still struggling with its demise today.

We are here challenged with no less than the liberation of the masculine and feminine "principles" in the lives of both men and women, and not only in economic roles and social prerogatives. These twins represent the changing masculine and feminine principles inside all of us. We are glimpsing them in the nascent stage of their development, just as they are being freed from dominance by the ruling power of patriarchal conventions. Apparently that began to happen very subtly in the high Gothic period. But it has come to full flower in our own age, where we must recognize it and allow it to transform our lives.

As our historic attitudes in Western Christian civilization have been predominantly patriarchal and masculine, the secondary position of the feminine has not only been a social phenomenon. More important, the feminine psychological tendencies in each person have been devalued and forced under the heel of masculine prejudices. This is just as true in women's own psyches as it is in men's. It would be a grievous mistake to understand this dilemma merely on the sociological or cultural level of women's rights.

In modern language we could say that the feminine principle fosters feeling, empathy, love, compassion, delight, joy, mystery, intimacy, playfulness, the primacy of human relationship, and the rhythms of nature. The feminine is particularly concerned with respecting and celebrating the innocent integrity of natural impulses and urges, and the immediate rapture of "aliveness." It brings us that wonderful experience we call bliss. The feminine gives us the dynamically receptive capacity to function as a vessel or container of life, in a spiritual and psychological manner as well as materially. It gives us our capacity to simply *be* in depth, and to accept ourselves naturally as we are.

Intimacy is a primary capacity of the feminine. The Latin *intimus* means "inmost" or "deepest." This suggests that true relatedness between persons is not merely a surface experience of close proximity. It is not a "cozying up" together. It is rather our mysterious entrance into a shared experience at a remarkably deeper level. Here our separateness no longer imprisons, and we are able to acknowledge and experience our common source in universal human nature. The feminine shows us how and where we are all essentially one. For this reason, the feminine has always fostered integration and peace.

In the mythic world of ancient Greece, Psyche was a young maiden who was wed to Eros, the god of love. This marriage symbolized the evolution of love, awareness, and creativity beyond the merely biological sexual impulse to a level of a conscious inner experience. The Greek word *psukhe* means "breath," "life," or "soul." The "psyche" in our modern world represents the feminine principle that gives us the containing "interiority" of ourselves, our sense of "soul." It also gives us that vital energy for living that seems to rise within us when we are inspired. It is in direct tension with the masculine principle that often defines our more conscious, exterior, worldly, and concrete social experience far beyond personal relationships and inner spiritual events.

Masculinity has a tendency to impress an abstract and idealized form onto what it conceives to be the raw material of nature.

It does this through organization, planning, legalization, reason, logic, discipline, and morality. The masculine principle of spirit, when it is firm but not oppressive, transforms nature into culture. But the feminine attempts to discern and live according to the inherent structure or patterns that are built into nature from the start. "Be yourself more fully here and now, accept yourself, and experience yourself in depth" is the feminine's approach to living. "Succeed," "Win," "Analyze and understand," "Make something better," or "Strive for perfection" is the masculine equivalent. Each is a one-sided fragment of the whole truth.

When these masculine and feminine principles unite in an encounter of mutual respect and value, a radiant new consciousness is formed that renews the vitality of any individual life or civilization.

The major inclination of Western civilization since the abolition of pagan antiquity has been the extreme and one-sided insistence upon the masculine extraverted and perfectionistic approach. The impulses and characteristics of nature and the feminine have often been not only relegated to second rank but even equated with the very snares of the Devil himself! From the first centuries of Christianity down to the present day, women have often been portrayed mythically and actually as sensual seductresses, archetypally epitomizing the worldly source of indolence, dissipation, and sin.

The feminine themes of nature, matter (from Latin *mater*, "mother"), pleasure, contentment, and well-being have been characterized—sometimes with good reason—as dangerous illusions. They were believed to lead the unwary from the stainless path of a virtuous and pure life. In the patriarchate, one must continue to strive ever higher for perfection.

What is most important is that, in our Western world, the feminine value and authority of inner psychological experience as a real source of truth and meaning have been greatly diminished. Reliance on this source was replaced by an extraverted "problem solving" approach within an organizational mindset.

In short, our *psychology* issues from the feminine principle, while our *sociology* is the product of a masculine perspective.

In the religious arena, an appreciation of the interiority of the soul, and of the feminine vessel in each of us, has been superseded by "group process" and a task-oriented stance. This stresses social work, "relevant" political activity, "leadership," and intellectual scholarship. Our religious institutions are still unwittingly governed by a masculine abstract, programmatic, and sociological outlook which ignores the inner world of real psychological and spiritual events within the vessel of the soul. These regions of human experience are left to mental health experts who trivialize matters of the spirit within their largely materialistic, pathological, and reductionistic frame of reference. The voice of God spoken in the depths of the soul is a severe threat to "normality" and to an adequate social adjustment. Most therapists personalize and relativize such experiences, thereby rendering them harmless. Ironically, most clergy are just as reductionistic and pathologically minded in their judgments.

There is, however, a valid reason for sometimes discouraging and devaluing impulsiveness and the tendency to live according to fantasy and dream wisdom. For it is indeed possible for a tender and vulnerable ego consciousness to be sucked back into a passive state of infantile reverie and wishful irresponsibility, which may even lead to serious psychic illness.

Before the modern era, the anima of men was lived out almost exclusively through projections onto actual women or through religious contemplation of the great goddess in one form or another. There was a tendency for women to set aside their own native femininity when it came time to relate to men, in favor of playing a social role that conveniently reflected the anima side of men. In modern times, certain women have become sex goddesses for millions—or, in a more domestic context, the television sit-com rendition of the perfect mother.

Of course this erotic idealization of women has pleased and

fascinated men, and at the same time has given women a certain seductive proprietary power over their men, which they learned to manipulate to their own advantage. But in so doing, women have acted as their own worst enemies.

For the real femininity of an actual woman and the anima of a man are remarkably different. The anima of a man is an interior archetypal presence that, when he is consciously aware of it, connects him to the deeper mystery and wholeness of his life and being. But this exotic inner woman is not part of the man's masculine consciousness in outer reality. His inner anima has no knowledge or sense of the outer world at all.

If a man were to unwittingly follow the impulses or dictates of his anima femininity, without any conscious masculine stability, discrimination, or judgment, he would make an utter fool of himself. He would be "loony," possessed by his "moon" femininity. He would be seduced or goaded back into an infantile and dreaming unconsciousness, carried away by his fantasies, and subject to the whimsical moods and reveries of his Mother Nature within—the darkly unconscious psyche.

When a man loses his masculine standpoint in consciousness, through passivity, fatigue, fear, or hurt feelings, and is unconsciously gripped by his anima energy, he falls into an extremely sensitive mood. He becomes passive, unreasonable, depressed, sentimental, imperious, irritable, resentful, "picky," "bitchy," "touchy," manically enthusiastic, or sophomorically idealistic. These moods may appear as overwhelmingly positive or negative, but a man is always impossible to live with under such circumstances. He is virtually "somewhere else." He is absent from true relationship in his role as spouse or father. Where is he?

His masculinity has disappeared. It has been swallowed by the power of his unconscious femininity. He is imprisoned in the vessel of his anima. He is conjugally joined to his mother complex. This inner mother dominates and subdues his real masculine feeling like an omnipotent goddess. Such a man has been seduced and "castrated," not by his wife or his lover, but by a part of his own unconscious psyche. He has only himself to blame. But he desperately needs help. He doesn't know how he feels. The only recourse is for him to take responsibility. He must get a conscious grip on his masculine standpoint. He must decide how he feels and what his attitude is, not out of his weak moodiness, but from his best alert judgment in the clarity of his mind and the honesty of his heart.

On the other hand, the innate femininity of an actual woman is a powerful source of love, intelligence, and practicality in down-to-earth reality, for a woman is dominantly and consciously feminine. Unlike a man, her mood connects her to reality, often to what is needed or required in the atmosphere or arrangements of living at a given moment. A woman's mood connects her to relationship. Her capacity for feminine love, nurture, empathy, support, reassurance, patience, compassion, sensuous intimacy, tender understanding, appreciation, acknowledgment, and acceptance are not luxuries, augmentations, or enrichments; they are the *central* necessities of life and are evidence of as much strength and genius as any man's heroic feat or intellectual coup. It is the prevailing masculine attitude in our culture that categorizes such talents as merely passive, instinctive, domestic, or personal, thereby taking them for granted and rendering them "easy" or inferior to what it conceives to be first-rate masculine capabilities.

The authoritative teaching of our tale is this: it is the masculine principle (in women and men) that is the initiating principle of highly focused and creative consciousness, the teacher, the authoritative transmitter of living tradition, transformer of nature and creator of culture, initiator of the young into the life of society, and guardian and disseminator of truth. The masculine articulates the meaning and significance of life, makes the rules, and administers them. The masculine principle, we might say, is all about the subject matter and the organizational policies and standards of life. It takes the raw material of natural existence and does something with it, makes something out of it, orders it, makes sense of it, illuminates it. The masculine is the active leader, who personifies initiative.

Women have access to the masculine spirit in variations of what Jung has called the Wise Old Man archetype. This evolves when a woman works seriously on the development of her animus capabilities, rather than living out this archetypal dimension vicariously through her relations with men. It is in this area that a "virgin birth" may occur within the soul of a woman, giving her an independent masculine capability, real freedom, a spiritual alertness, cerebral acuteness, and true individuality.

"I was alone in my own room," dreamt a sixteen-year-old girl just after her first counseling session, "and the window was partly open, when all of a sudden a seagull flew right in. He and I strangely seemed to know and understand each other. Then in a minute he darted out again and was gone."

We can easily recognize this scene from the mythic inheritance of our Christian tradition as a variant of the Annunciation scene. Such a dream says that a powerful new psychological development is in store for this young lady. A masculine and spiritually inseminating visitor has just appeared from out of the depths of the unconscious. One need only wait for the conscious experience of a new development in this girl's life.

The feminine principle, as contrasted with the masculine (in both women *and* men, remember!), is life itself. It is the actual, down-to-earth, unidealistic, practical organic stuff of nature and matter. It is all the rich variety of creation, in the most direct and immediate experience of things and people as they are in fact, up close. The feminine principle is the spontaneous eruption of feeling and the bonding between persons. It is a world ruled by the heart, where love and devotion spring from a spontaneous and utterly free natural feeling. Love does not arise from obligation or commitment, or as a response to any didactic authority that is imposed sociologically or institutionally.

The feminine is life and love without power motives in complete and utter innocence. She can never be comprehended by rules, ideals, theories, job descriptions, or programs. The feminine principle is the ecstasy of being fully alive and "in touch." It is the water of life, the healing balm, utter wholeness and completeness. It is "home" and "belonging" to some person or place. It is presence, the arresting experience of life as life. It is beauty and the symbol of all fulfillment. When I stand somewhere, with no place to go and nothing I have to do, in a mundane and familiar spot, and say, "I am so glad and thankful to be alive," then I am in the intimate presence of the feminine principle at its best. Its wondrous cornucopia is overflowing in my lap faster than I can keep up with it.

The feminine is the "beingness" of actual life. The masculine is the knowing appreciation and realization of this deep mystery.

Our traditional masculine-oriented culture has accentuated men's subjective version of anima femininity as the universal standard of all femininity. We see this version clearly expressed in one of the biblical accounts of the Creation of human beings. [1] Adam is created first, then Eve is brought forth out of his side into her own separate existence. This emergence of Eve from Adam, a kind of birth event, suggests that actual woman's nature is modeled after the interior anima femininity of man and is not unique in its own right. This myth implies that there is no difference between the unconscious femininity of men and the conscious femininity of women.

Our religious heritage has led men to expect women to conform to men's own prejudicial and subjective expectations of feminine identity and behavior. One can see glaring examples of this version of "femininity" in advertising, in which glamorous or seductive goddesses provide the mystique and subliminal atmosphere for the products being promoted. Such a prostitution of actual women in order to manipulate and titillate the psyches of male consumers is an insult to the strong and intelligent femininity of real women. It's no wonder that many women have reacted against the "feminine" roles that the culture expects of them.

But since women themselves have been raised in the same patriarchal atmosphere, they too have tended to adopt a male version of anima femininity in their own lives, without exactly knowing what they were doing. It isn't completely true that women have been forced to do this sociologically by dominant male authorities. It is just as true to say that the male domination has come from within the unconscious inner male of women—the animus personality—to which they have naively acquiesced.

It is the unconscious animus side of a woman that is so subtly affected by one-sided patriarchal values. These she assimilates psychologically from her father and from the animus of her mother, and other male authorities of her early cultural experiences. In this circumstance, women bear an equal responsibility with men for patriarchal, male-dominated values and prejudices. Both men and women are the causes and the victims of masculine one-sidedness. Mothers, too, may unconsciously instill chauvinistic patriarchal values and patterns in both sons and daughters, even ostensibly in the name of feminism or "unisex" equality. Most of us today still judge the competence of a liberated person according to conventional masculine criteria. In this scheme of things, feminine characteristics are subtly depreciated and devalued, so that women are encouraged to become imitation men.

When a woman identifies with her animus, most of her conscious femininity shrinks to zero, and in its place appears a strident, aggressive, pseudo-rational, opinionated, hypertalkative, inflexible, overintellectual, preachy, censorious, priggish, argumentative, unrelated, prejudiced, power-hungry *man*, vested in the surface costume of a woman's body. Even other women have a tough time with such a creature. Most men find it impossible to relate to her. To men, it seems as if they have but two choices, either to crush her with brute male force or to withdraw immediately beyond her range. The second is generally a safer and more effective choice.

Women of the upper classes often tend to cloak their animus behind a smokescreen of well-bred manners and polite "tact."

But lurking beneath their genteel persona is a steel claw of power and cold, tactical manipulation, which they use to run the affairs of everyone else's life.

Women with an extreme animus problem do not necessarily inflict it on other people. Sometimes they turn it against themselves. They quietly suffer and are torn to pieces by their own callous self-criticism, doubts, persistent thoughts of inadequacy and unworthiness, despair, and the fateful expectation that nothing will ever change for the better. Women who finally commit suicide are often plagued with such an animus problem. The strong, life-giving, and sustaining femininity that might have rescued them from the animus' steel grip long ago fell victim to his stealthy brainwashing and incessant cruelty. Our patriarchal culture encourages women to fall into this insidious trap.

Whether an animus-possessed woman spreads her terror around the neighborhood or keeps it suffocatingly to herself, her femininity is always passive. The swaggering, aggressive, dominating, opinionated, and sharp-tongued woman is really not present in her femininity. What one observes is the animus itself, running roughshod over her weak and acquiescing feminine consciousness. Such women always feel shy, incompetent, ineffective, and insubstantial inside themselves, and haven't the slightest notion of how they appear from another's point of view. It is useless to attempt an argument with the animus, for he will simply raise the ante and fight back even harder. He is generally more interested in power and domination than in truth or genuine relationship. One must talk directly to the woman herself. Naturally, this requires a certain skill.

One must never tell an animus woman to be softer, quieter, or more ladylike. This will only make her femininity even weaker and the animus more dominant. The best way for a woman to handle a bad animus attack is to screw up her confidence, take herself firmly in hand, and decide *for herself* exactly how she feels, what she thinks, and what she expects to do as a woman about something or other in the practical world. At this point she needs to stay clear of abstract theories and contemporary stereotypes about what it means to be "liberated." She must give herself lots of permission to exercise the strongest feminine judgment and love she can muster in down-to-earth reality. Then the negative animus evaporates in an instant, though probably not for too long.

One thing is certain: *someone* will take charge! The question is, will it be an unprejudiced, free, and deliberately conscious woman, or her unconscious and autonomous animus? The animus always flows in where the conscious woman is passive or distracted, or when her energies are sapped and she has trouble coping.

I once observed a family scene on the sidewalk in front of a country restaurant. It was picture-taking time, and the mother had the camera. Her husband and adult son sat on the seat of an old carriage. Nothing the husband or son did in the way of posing seemed to please this woman. "Do this!" "Look there!" "Smile this way!" "No, not that way!" "Put your legs over there!" "No, not like that!" and so forth. As I quietly stood near this exasperated photographer, she became increasingly impatient and irritated. Then she seemed to catch herself, abruptly stopped shouting, looked down, and mumbled to herself, "Why don't you shut up, Janet, and just take the picture!" Such a remarkable assertion of feminine consciousness over so bossy an animus made my heart leap for joy. It took great courage for that woman to do what she did. She got hold of herself and stood up to the animus. She made a conscious assessment of the situation and decided that her impatient and bossy impulses were inappropriate, inconsiderate, condescending, and impractical.

Women have often set their own feminine traits aside, for which they find precious little resonance in the environment, and have substituted a kind of artificial femininity that they suspected a man would value or love. This is playacting and a childish form of flirtatious imitation designed to give women an ego boost, a sense of security, and a seductive influence on men. It is done for the sake of gaining some kind of power and control, but it does grave damage to their real femininity and to the principle of love.

When a woman gives up her own femininity in order to align herself with a man's anima, she is giving up *conscious related-ness*. Relatedness is a realistic connection between two or more persons or spheres of influence. It is the opposite of *identifica-tion*. When a woman "plays up" to a man, she flirtatiously identifies herself with his unconscious feminine side. From the man's point of view it feels as if there is an almost heavenly merging of their separate selves into one. This phenomenon is not an interpersonal relationship at all, but essentially an intraper-sonal erotic fusion. It is like a bewitching spell. Its purpose is to effect a power-seduction for ulterior motives. It is a form of displaced incest.

In this circumstance, a woman senses the man's expectations, which stem from his anima. "You be soft and gentle but not too smart or aggressive," or "You find out what I want and give it to me before I even have to ask," or "You manage my private life, and arrange the atmosphere so that I can relax and forget all my problems," or "You praise me and make me feel like a strong and important man," or "You drop everything and be there exactly when, where, and as I need you." Such a woman is identifying herself with the man's anima-mother complex. Does she really desire to make an incestuous connection to the man by playing the erotic mother to him? For some women the answer is yes, for this is precisely their feline weapon that may win them power over and possession of a man.

Men do something similar. They sense the ideal expectations of men that come from the woman's animus and attempt to play this role. At first they learn to do this in relation to their mothers, and then it shifts to other women as they grow older. "You do the thinking for both of us," or "You be strong and courageous," or "You know how to fix this or organize that and make everything work," or "You become a big success and provide for us and protect us," are typical animus projections from the woman. A man often feels that he must live up to these expectations if he is to be a competent male. In other words, he will try to be the woman's incestuous father. This tactic may give a man control and possession over a woman and keep her a child. He will become her erotic father and guardian.

Deep down in their hearts, neither men nor women feel completely comfortable playing these subliminally assigned and induced roles. It doesn't leave them much freedom to be their own real or whole selves in relation to one another. Playing anima or animus is almost always a form of seduction, power-mongering, and manipulation, whether they realize it or not. Such people are flirtatiously playing god and goddess to each other as they cross the tabooed boundaries of psychological incest.

But more shortsightedly, this is also the stuff of romance and love affairs, which often start off as pure bliss but may quickly end up as intensely negative. Certain healthy inner resistances begin to interfere with the illusory roles that each partner expects the other to play. A man and a woman simply get tired of conforming to the projected images, and they prove to be incapable of doing it well enough to satisfy their partner's unrealistic expectations.

In our story, the death of the duke and duchess have left the masculine and feminine impulses on their own, with no traditional or objective authority to guide them. We actual men and women now feel battered by these archetypal forces that are trying to make themselves heard in our own lives today.

FOUR

THE COVER-UP

IT comes as a great shock to the twins when the sister discovers that she is pregnant. They are at a loss as to what to do.

Then the brother says he knows of an extremely wise man, one who had been the late duke's closest advisor. Before the duke's death, he had recommended this man in the event the children needed help. Perhaps this advisor can find a solution to their predicament. They summon him to the palace immediately.

When the old baron arrives, the twins tell him of the secret matter that is so shameful to them. They are afraid of losing all honor and good reputation unless he can help them find a solution. They kneel at his feet, utterly distressed, and earnestly appeal to him. They wish to know where the sister can be concealed so that no one will learn about the child. The boy says he thinks he ought to go somewhere far away until this matter can be resolved.

After prudent consideration, their late father's wise counselor gives them the following advice. First, the young duke should call his leading barons to court and announce his intention of making a religious pilgrimage to the grave of Christ in the Holy Land. Second, he must request that the barons make a pledge of fealty to his sister to be their liege lady, so that she may rule in his stead. Then the old counselor advises him to go on the pilgrimage and repent of his great sin. Third, after the brother has left, the sister should accompany the wise baron to his own estates, where she can be secretly entrusted to his care and protection. There she will undergo her confinement and bear her child away from all prying eyes. After the birth, the sister should keep her station in life, rule her lands, and use such material means as she possesses to atone for her sin by acts of mercy and service to the poor.

The day quickly arrives when the brother and sister have to part company. They have been so inseparable all their lives that they feel they are exchanging their hearts, one to the other. When the brother departs, he leaves his heart with his dear sister, and although she stays behind, her heart travels away with him.

The sister-duchess is taken into the care and protection of the old counselor and his wife, and some months later the youthful duchess gives birth to a little son who is sweeter and more wonderful than anyone can possibly imagine.

But what is to be done with this child? He doesn't belong anywhere. He has no legitimate place anywhere in the world. He is a misfit. His inheritance goes sideways. He is the product of the worst sin imaginable! His parents dare not claim him as their own.

Neither the duchess nor the baron nor his wife can bring themselves to kill the infant. But after some consideration, the old baron advises the duchess to place him completely in the hands of God. He recommends that they abandon the child to the sea, taking all necessary precautions to promote his survival.

Secretly, the baron finds a sturdy chest and a small boat. These are made ready. The young mother deposits many yards of the richest silk brocade material in the chest, twenty marks of pure gold, and an exquisite ivory tablet, framed in gold and encrusted with precious stones, upon which she writes of the child's rank and the highly irregular circumstances of his conception.

She records that the boy is being sent away in order to hide the sinful love between a brother and sister who are his true parents. She hopes that whoever finds the boy, presuming that God preserves and protects him, will see to it that he is properly baptized and will use the gold judiciously to pay for his upbringing in a safe place. She advises that the treasure be increased through wise investment.

The mother hopes that the boy will eventually be taught to read and that this tablet will be carefully preserved for him, so that one day he might read it for himself, which will free him from arrogance. It might be his good fortune to grow up a virtuous man and dedicate his life to God, thereby to atone constantly, with loving filial duty, for his parents' heinous sin.

In recording all of this, the young duchess does not mention the child's family name or country of origin, for his own good.

When all is in readiness, the little boy and his precious tablet are placed gently in the chest with the silk and the gold. The chest is securely closed and tightly lashed into the small boat. After nightfall, this little skiff is pushed gently out onto the ebbing tide, and the little captain floats away and is in God's hand.

Our tale says that the twins are afraid of losing all honor and reputation if the girl's pregnancy is discovered. They call upon their father's old and trusted counselor to find a way of hiding and disposing of the cause of their shame. This is reminiscent of the sister's feeling when her brother abused her in the middle of the night. She was about to cry out for help but realized that if they were discovered together, *they would lose all good fame and honor.*

It seems apparent that the "shame" that the twins feel has

more to do with the tarnishing of their glorious reputation than it does with any real guilt or sense of responsibility. This is the way with inflation. It takes a simple and down-to-earth human being to experience conscious guilt. The twins have assumed the archetype of the divine marriage, so they are far beyond any merely human sensitivity or responsibility. They have the unassailable reputation of God to protect! Their child, which symbolizes the possibility of a new and creative life, is less important to them than their reputation. Their self-esteem is based not upon a consciousness of their inner psychological roots, but upon how other people judge them.

It is striking how the young mother abandons her child to the sea in order to protect this reputation. Our tale mentions not the slightest resistance or hesitation on her part. In normally healthy women, motherhood is an unusually powerful force, and the need to protect and nourish her child can easily dominate every other instinct in a woman's life. Deep inside a mother lurks a tigress. She will rise to ferocity in order to protect her cub. It therefore appears very odd that the young mother relinquishes her child to almost certain death alone on the sea. Something in her maternal instinct is amiss. Also, by abandoning her child, she is cutting off all possibilities of individuation that the child represents. Symbolically, she is rejecting the Divine Child archetype. This distressing inadequacy in the lady's femininity is a key symptom of the moralistic sway of patriarchal conventions, to which she has succumbed.

According to Jung, the Divine Child is born out of the womb of the unconscious psyche. It is begotten out of the depths of human nature, and is not the product of interpersonal love relations. It is a gift from Nature herself, as she responds to the Spirit. Psychologically, the Divine Child is a personification of vital forces that lie outside the range of the conscious mind. Such a phenomenon represents ways and possibilities of living that our ordinary consciousness knows nothing about. It is a wholeness that embraces the very depths of nature. The Divine Child expresses the strongest and most relentless urge in every being, the urge to realize itself. This urge to self-realization is a veritable law of nature. It is of invincible power, even though it may seem small and insignificant—even improbable, when its effects are felt initially.[1]

The Divine Child is a dimension of the central archetype of the Self. It is the leading edge of the Self's development. In real life, the parents' projection of the Divine Child image onto their own actual child is what makes that little person seem so particularly sweet and adorable and precious to them. It is also what lends to the child that quality of fatefulness and great promise: a future life ready to unfold in all its mystery. It is part of the instinct of parenthood, which resides in every adult human being. This is released or catalyzed by pregnancy and the birth of a baby. When we look at a little vulnerable and defenseless child, a strong feeling sweeps over us. We can hardly resist reaching out and enfolding the child in our arms. We are automatically drawn to the little one and crave to be protective and physically embracing. Our instincts arrange for us to relate to a child in this way. Many of us respond similarly to small domestic mammals. It is just "in our blood" to be like this. It is an animal feeling. This is archetypal behavior.

But our young mother does not feel these instincts very strongly. She wants to cover up her pregnancy and protect her reputation. The archetype of the Divine Child is in trouble somewhere within this woman. Her maternal responses are too weak.

The Divine Child symbolizes the future potential for creative development, what Jung has called the individuation process, in the womb-depths of human nature. It is the growth and development of that universal and archetypal dimension of our personalities that fulfills our deeper and larger destiny as human beings. It represents the possibility for psychic wholeness. This is the sublime gift of the feminine principle in all our lives.

The offspring of the twins' union seems to represent the ultimate possibility of unique wholeness and integrity of which a human life is capable. He is the product of a union of opposites, untainted by the common values of collective-mindedness. He represents integration. But the young parents are incapable of taking responsibility for this in their lives. Like the Christ of the New Testament, this little boy turns out to be "the stone which was rejected."[2]

Every child is a little god to its parents, which is why they dote upon the little creature with such abandon. But such an archetype must ultimately function *within the interior life of the parent* if psychological development in the parent's own life is to occur. This is the meaning for us of the twins' child. By abandoning her child, the young duchess is failing to take responsibility for her own individuation process. To send the boy away on the sea is to repress the archetype of the Divine Child.

This sweet little boy, the fruit of the incestuous union between the brother and sister twins, is a horrible embarrassment to them. He is the glaring evidence of their sin. Any future life for this boy within the realm is thought to be impossible. He can have no secure position or legitimate status in that world. Sweet though he is, he is a misfit, an incongruous and untenable being: an outcast.

This is how children feel when they are abandoned by their parents either literally or psychologically. To themselves they seem to say, "If I were good enough and lovable enough, then they wouldn't have left, or they would have found me more interesting and would have cared for me. It's all my fault. There's something wrong with me!"

The outcast mentality goes hand in hand with the perfectionism of patriarchal values. If the Devil, the human capacity for sin, is utterly alien to human nature as God created it, and if evil is the dualistic opposite of good, then the things that make us respond to evil must be excised—cut out—and unilaterally rejected. "And if your eye should cause you to sin, tear it out."[3]

But if *wholeness* rather than perfectionism is the measure of a successful and complete life, then we must acknowledge, consciously deal with, and ultimately accept every aspect of our being, including all negative tendencies, as potentially healthy ingredients of the personality. Our modern society has unwittingly repressed evil and sin, making it a split-off aspect of our wholeness. In a most facile way, we say that we simply don't believe in evil or sin anymore, as if that could eliminate our antiquated moralism. Evil has therefore gained unconscious power over us and functions in a one-sidedly negative or destructive way. That is why censorship and the "don'ts" of fundamentalistic thought have been so prevalent. We believe that through will, discipline, and "right thinking," we can keep the shadow side of our existence at bay or eliminate it completely.

One of the central paradoxes of our tale is that this little boy, born of incest, will eventually become a great holy man and teacher and will lead others to wholeness and holiness. But he is being rejected by his parents precisely because he is a misfit, a product of the most odious sin. We are being taught here that the truth and completeness of our own lives first appear to us as something hideous and sinful, something of which we desperately want to rid ourselves. Jung frequently warned his students that good often appears first in our consciousness in the guise of evil.

Such a paranoid attitude about the darker side of the human character has led us to attempt various methods of ridding ourselves of thoughts or impulses that are distasteful, frightening, embarrassing, or incongruous. If the dark side seems to have turned up in the form of another person, then he is immediately made the scapegoat and is accordingly either punished or rejected. This allows the perfectionistic attitude to rule supreme.

The Holocaust in Nazi Germany was an abominable example of this perfectionistic streak in our Western consciousness, carried to psychotic proportions. The German fascist mentality was bent upon ridding the "pure Aryan race" of everything it considered weak, inferior, and deficient. Six million Jewish and Romany (Gypsy) men, women, and children, together with numerous handicapped persons and suspected homosexuals—all of whom represented ethnic or psychological inferiority to the Nazis—were gassed or shot to death and then cremated. These people had been forced to become the scapegoats for what Germany could not face in itself. Hitler accused the Jews of over-zealous ambition and money-mongering, but it was he himself who tried to lead Germany to world domination through blatant and systematic exploitation and deceit. In his cold fanaticism, he did not hesitate to employ distortion, divisive fabrication, unbridled ruthlessness, terror, violence, and murder, in order to attain his ends. As a recent *New York Times* retrospective editorial put it, "Hitler stands alone in the history of villainy." Whenever we insist on our perfectionism to the exclusion of our apparent inferiorities or limitations, we are playing Hitler to ourselves. It is inflation that lies behind our perfectionistic traits.

The twins see themselves as having made a terrible mistake that is extremely inconvenient from the point of view of their political responsibilities and reputation. So they follow the advice of the old counselor and cover it up. They have made firm resolutions. From now on they are going to be *good*. And the child of their *badness* has been eliminated. But the child of their badness will be the chief hero of the tale.

Jung used to say that a good attitude can always lead to some evil, and darkest evil to some good. This expresses the psychological paradox that any extreme position has an inherent tendency to flip into its own opposite.

That which seems evil to the twins has been abandoned to the wilds of the sea. The theme of the abandonment (traditionally termed "exposure") of a noble or auspicious child is very common in folklore and mythology. It was actually practiced in ancient times. Often this was done because the child was considered to be a threat to the well-being of the realm, or it was feared that he might eventually come to overthrow the government and seize power himself.

The young Oedipus was exposed in the barren countryside in an attempt to frustrate an oracular forecast that he would grow up that he would grow up to murder his father, the king of Thebes, and then marry his mother.

In ancient Troy, it was told that the young boy Paris was exposed because his pregnant mother dreamt that she would give birth to a firebrand that would consume Troy.

While the future Cyrus the Great was still in utero, his maternal grandfather dreamed that his daughter gave birth first to a gigantic flood and then to a prodigious vine, both of which overpowered all of Asia. Owing to fear of this prognostication, the infant Cyrus was exposed to probable death in the wilderness.[4]

These legends concerning the infancy of persons who eventually turned out to live heroic or fateful lives seems to say that when destiny is at work in bringing in a new epoch or revolutionary period, the conventional ruling father-powers will do everything imaginable to thwart such a new development.

It is virtually the same in our own lives. Whenever it is necessary or possible for an individual to develop further in psychological awareness, the first thing that happens is an enormous resistance. "I'm scared to death!" "This is utter foolishness!" "I can't possibly do it!" "It's totally crazy and irresponsible." "Do you think I'm insane?" "Now I'm sure it's time to stop therapy." Such a person pleads every excuse in the book and then some.

I once knew a man who told me that over the course of his life he had developed a fool-proof test about how to make good decisions. Whenever he felt absolutely and uncritically sure and confident about something, he interpreted this as a sign of danger and accordingly exercised the utmost caution. But when he felt a nagging sense of fear and a subtle desire to run away from a task or challenge, he knew he was exactly on the right track. He would then push through his fear and reluctance with as much courage and good sense as he could muster.

Jung observed that whenever a person had hit upon a really new and creative possibility for living—a real invitation to profound development—instantly, all the negative forces would come charging in from all points of the compass and try to squelch it. In the course of good psychotherapy, such a sudden and intense resistance or anxiety is a virtual confirmation that important new and unfamiliar ground is being struck in the life of the person, of which he or she is understandably afraid.

This resistance demonstrates that a really vital and revolutionary advancement is in the wings. The psychological equivalent of destiny, fate, or divine Providence is exerting its aim within a person's life. This contributes to the growth and evolutionary development of the personality, which Jung termed the individuation process. It invariably produces a negative reaction on the part of the limited ego consciousness. Much of our anxiety stems from our fear of our own selves.

So there are great things in store for the baby as he is abandoned to the sea and to God.

Unfortunately, the baby is considered only in his outward significance. This is typical of the patriarchal mind, which has a penchant for taking inner and symbolic truths and applying them or understanding them in a purely literal and concrete manner.

"What would people say?" is the gnawing question that so often arises when we contemplate following our own integrity and deeper truth, or sacrificing it for the sake of a comfortable adjustment to esteemed reputation and conformity. Parents have been known to disown their children and individuals have stifled their very impulses to creative adventure, all for the sake of "reputation." The impulse to new life is never approved of at first. It always appears to be a dangerous threat to safe "normality."

The twins request guidance from their late father's trusted counselor, and when he arrives, they kneel at his feet and appeal to him for help. In a sense, this old counselor functions as a father substitute to them. Therefore he represents the old patriarchal world that is passing away. Whatever it is that is developing in the course of the twins' strange predicament, it will no doubt receive a cool reception at the hands of this scion of the old masculine conventions.

In the outer world their little boy will appear to represent the negative side of *sacer*, not the sacred, holy, or consecrated, but the accursed and horrible. He will be seen to be of the Devil, not of God.

Our tale has come to this deplorable and irresolvable impasse because an inner reality—the possibility of a union of opposites—has been lived out concretely and literally, rather than being experienced symbolically. Instead of coming to terms with the dark side of the psyche, the twins have simply acted out the devilish impulse unconsciously.

It is well worth noting the difference between *experience* and *expression*. Our vulgar, literalistic mentality persuades us that we must have an actual, physical encounter with a person, situation, or thing in order to have any valid experience of reality. Something we can't encounter outwardly with one or more of the five senses simply doesn't exist for us!

But our entire experience of inward reality, that which is psychological, comes to us one way or another, indirectly through metaphor and symbol. The prefix *meta-* in Greek refers to a change of place, order, condition, or nature. The syllable *phor* means "to bear" or "carry." Therefore, a metaphor transfers an idea or a meaning from one object to another, so that the second object carries the meaning of the first object. This suggests that we experience ourselves and the deeper archetypal reality that lies within us in an indirect and therefore nonliteral fashion. Just as we have physical eyes to see and ears to hear, we humans also have intuitive "organs" within our psyche to pick up and work with metaphorical messages about reality, and our outer lives benefit immeasurably when we do.

The twins can't deal with their sinfulness except on the literal level of actual behavior. This precludes insight or reflection. They have no experience of themselves interiorly. They can't learn from valuing their sinful impulses as inner ingredients oftheir own character. They can't separate their actual behavior from their inherent capability or potential for sin.

This discrimination of inward reflection from actual behavior is one of the tasks of our infant hero. He will bring us that precious and powerful capability called *consciousness*. But this is beyond the capacity of his parents, who live in the relatively simple patriarchal world of right and wrong, good and evil, where all is concrete and definite, and a literalistic code of inflexible values is decided for all time.

So the beautiful newborn boy is sent away, exiled from the land of his parents. He has become an outcast. The rejection of this child from the shores of his own land suggests that he is being pushed back into the unconscious. There he will eventually fall victim to projection. This is a good example of how projection is defined by psychologists as a "defense mechanism." Some unacceptable or devalued content of the personality rises toward consciousness. But since it is incompatible with standard moral and ethical values, or with one's favorite self-image, it is dismissed before it can put in a decent appearance.

This very dismissal often takes the form of a displacement or projection of the content away from one's self and out somewhere into the surrounding world, where it eventually turns up as the apparent character trait or motivation of some other person. A neighbor or a person of one's acquaintance appears irritatingly inferior to us or seems to display repulsive moral traits, motivations, or values. We get a certain thrill out of despising him, and this relieves us of any culpability of our own. He's the despicable one, and we're that much more comfortable and satisfied with ourselves.

The mother sends the child away with a note asking someone else to take responsibility. She hopes that her child will be lucky enough to be rescued by others somewhere across the sea.

How often do we unwittingly demand that others take on what we are unwilling or unable to accept and cope with in the homeland of our own selves? But such dishonest machinations always come back to haunt us one way or another. In the end we can never escape a psychological content whose time has come.

Circumstances have a cleverly ironic way of bringing our maneuverings back home again to roost, so that we are finally stuck with ourselves for good or ill.

Nonetheless, since the twins have put the child "in God's hands," it will be interesting to see what transpires. Often our defensive motives and clever psychological maneuverings end up producing a result that is quite different from what we expect.

Ralph Waldo Emerson said that we should be cautious about what requests we make of God, because we may get precisely what we ask for, but at a time or under circumstances in which we may bitterly regret our original petition.

FIVE

LOVE AND DEATH

SEPARATED from her brother and her son, the young mistress of the realm now suffers from three sorrows. She has sinned with her own brother and has had to part from him. She suffers in her body the pain and exhaustion of childbirth. And she is beginning to have second thoughts about having consigned her little son to the rough and wild sea.

Then, a few days later, a fourth sorrow is added to the first three: word reaches her that her dear brother has died on his way to the Holy Land. His love for his twin sister has been so intense that, parted from her, he has fallen victim to love-sickness. Its violent and hungry sting has sent him on the road to death. In longing for her, he has died of a broken heart.

The most intense grief and mourning descend upon the beautiful duchess like a dark and angry cloud.

As soon as it becomes publicly known that the duke is dead

and that this young, beautiful, and unmarried noblewoman is the ruler of the land, eager suitors appear. They come from far and wide, seeking her hand in marriage. The duchess's great wealth and the charm and loveliness of her person make her an excellent prospect for many a neighboring prince.

But a cold and intractable resolution fills the duchess's breast. This aristocratic young lady rejects every single proposal. She announces that she has no intention whatsoever of marrying *any* mortal man!

"I have already chosen a mighty hero to be my husband," she exclaims one day, "a man who is dearer than any other in all the world—who has been loved since the beginning of time." In saying this, she refers to Jesus Christ, the Savior.

The lady misses no opportunity to court her Beloved by singing his praises night and day in her heart. She forswears all comfort and chastises her body through fasting, night vigils, and unceasing prayer, and by performing works of mercy without limit. She shows great remorse in an attempt to earn God's grace once again.

Not far away lives a lord who petitions repeatedly for her hand in marriage. When he has done everything in his power to persuade her to accept him, and she still adamantly refuses, he finally loses patience, and together with his knights and an army he invades her land, sacking the cities and strongholds. He continues to devastate her entire realm, right down to her one remaining citadel, behind whose walls she and her few remaining defenders barricade themselves.

The circumstances of this young woman's life are reduced to a wasteland of guilt, anxiety, and grief. The two persons whom she loves above all else are gone, and she fears the loss of God as well. To her it seems that she has been born to suffer. Life appears to have turned against her on all fronts.

This "wasteland" is the condition of the personality when it has been subjected to some form of violence. From our psychological perspective this violence does not always come from outside the personality, but often from within. It is the way in which we unwittingly treat ourselves, usually without understanding what we are doing.

Violence is "violation," a disregard of privacy or a desecrating of something special or sacred. The brother violated his sister by forcing her to have sex with him against her will. She allowed herself to be taken by him because she couldn't risk ruining her reputation. This same love continued in its violence until it killed the brother with love-sickness. Love turned upon him as death. The sister's reaction to the loss of her son and brother took the form of a violent impulse: her cold resolution to marry no mortal man and instead to devote herself to God in an extreme and torturing form of piety. She feared the violent reaction of God, who might damn her soul to hell for eternity. Then the suitor became violent when his love petitions were refused, and he invaded the duchess's realm by force and destroyed her cities and strongholds. So much violence!

We commit such "violent" acts on ourselves whenever we become inflated. As I noted earlier, inflation involves the lack of clear distinction between the ordinary human realm and the divine-archetypal level of the personality. Whenever we start "playing God" to ourselves or toward another person, we are committing a kind of violence. This generally happens when we make absolute and inflexible demands on ourselves or others, as if it were both our divine right and prerogative.

Whenever we assume that we *must* be a certain kind of person, accomplish something, or have something, we are being violent with ourselves. The chief symptoms are always an overpowering sense of necessity and omniscient "rightness," and a total absence of individual choice or balanced judgment. "The *only* thing I can do is . . . !" The excessive busyness of our lives and our inability to measure and conserve our use of physical and psychological energy is an expression of this problem of inflation. Because the rest of the psyche does not necessarily agree with the ego's assumptions, it is not long before intense conflict and a

resulting depression ensue. This is the wasteland. Such a wasteland is always filled with much striving and intensity, but very
little compassion or patience for the ordinary failings and limitations of our own selves as mere human creatures. We do violence
to ourselves whenever we fail to acknowledge and accept ourselves as we are. We also do such violence when we treat other
people in this way.

As we consider the sudden religiosity of the young and beautiful mistress of the realm, we are left with the distinct impression
that her zealous devotion to God is a displacement of her egotistical and inflated love for her deceased brother, and not a sincere
worship of the divine. The violent retribution that she expects
from God is less a real divine attribute than it is a manifestation of
the duchess's own violent self-interest. It never entered her heart
that God might have had compassion or love for her in her
predicament. She preempted God's judgment and was unsym-
pathetically severe with herself. Her contrition and remorse were
saturated with pride. In a way it is true to say that this young
woman doesn't know the difference between God and her own
negative animus. Her femininity has been dominated by a severe
patriarchal sense of justice. This was typical of the psychology of
the patriarchal period.

She repents her great sin and is afraid of what God will do to
her, but the fact remains that she has secretly disposed of the
evidence. She is practicing a dishonest cover-up to preserve the
appearance of perfection in the eyes of her subjects.

The sister behaves like an erotic snob. None of the suitors who
approach her is quite adequate. Since she can't have the one she
loves—or, rather, since she cooperated in banishing her loved
one to the Holy Land—there is no one in the world whom she
considers good enough. Only Jesus Christ, the incarnate God, is
worthy of her choice. This is a vastly inflated woman!

"Jesus Christ" is here functioning in the role of what Jungians
commonly call the ghostly lover animus.[1] A woman who is ob-
sessed and possessed by a romantic inner image of the ideal man

is never able to make a normal relation to an actual man in the form of a healthy relationship. Each time a male prospect enters her vicinity, such a woman immediately subjects him to all manner of extravagant and ideal comparisons. The poor fellow can never quite measure up, for the woman's criteria are simply not of this world. No man can be as perfect and as godlike as the one who seems to whisper so subtly in her deepest soul: "But of course there could be more, much more. Don't let yourself get stuck with this baboon who will only turn out to disappoint you. Keep looking, and eventually you will find *me*, your perfect match. Then it will be heaven!"

But such an incarnation of the deity never arrives, and if his semblance by hook or crook does seem to have appeared, you can be sure there will be trouble. Before long a most glaring and incompatible *fact* will show through the woman's projected illusion. It will not be long before she starts to complain that her perfect lover has "changed" for the worse. Of course, men do the same thing with women. It is simply another form of violence, arising from inflation.

The twin brother dies of love-sickness on his way to the Holy Sepulcher. The grave of Christ in the Holy Land was ostensibly the chief inspiration for the medieval Crusades. These military expeditions, sanctioned by the Church, attempted to recover the chief Christian shrines from Muslim control. The pilgrimages began in the late eleventh century and ended in the thirteenth. The historical setting of our tale coincides with the height of crusading fervor in the Middle Ages.

The Holy Sepulcher was the stone mausoleum where Christ was laid after his death on the cross. It was also the site of his believed resurrection from the dead. Thus, it embodied an awe-inspiring mystery: the utterly mysterious change from death to life. Nothing caught the fervor of the medieval religious imagination more than this. Resurrection! Even today, the mere thought of such an image carries considerable impact.

But there is a dark, negative side to the symbolism of the

grave. It represents the annihilation of consciousness by the power of the devouring feminine. In this context, death is the extinction of the individual and of consciousness as light.[2]

Symbolically speaking, a grave of stone or earth signifies the feminine or mother principle. Mother Earth gives birth to all life out of the death of the old season. The mythological focus of the ancient agrarian city-state cultures of the high Neolithic to Bronze Age period[3] was the ritualistic slaughter of animals and the death of vegetation in the autumn, which were always followed by a springtime of new life. A seed buried in the ground like a corpse sprouted to form a new season's growth. In similar fashion the Holy Sepulcher symbolizes a renewal and a transformation of the old into the new by a process of death and resurrection.

The problem at this stage of our tale is that there has been a displacement of the offering of one's self to God to an erotic "in-love" encounter on the personal, human plane. The twin brother made a goddess of his sister—an act of idolatry. Therefore he could not experience the spiritual transformation of death and rebirth in his own being. While consciousness is stuck in outer romance, spiritual transformation can only be negative—that is, it can only be understood literally as the finality of death and decay, followed by the promise of a new life in the hereafter, but without any vision or possibility of renewal in one's present existence. This explains why the brother's pilgrimage failed. He couldn't let go of his egoistic and inflated attachment to his sister. The attitude that the brother represented needed to be sacrificed so that further development could occur.

The old duke's trusted counselor advised the brother to leave his realm and make a pilgrimage to the Holy Sepulcher. But he died on his travels at about the same time that the son was born to his twin sister. When a death and a birth happen simultaneously in a story, the significance is a change of psychic energy from one form to another. Apparently the new will succeed where the old was incapable of functioning satisfactorily. We must watch for this as the tale unfolds. The son will achieve something that the father failed to accomplish. Perhaps he will turn out to be less "violent" in his affections. He will be less one-sidedly patriarchal.

Thematically, intense romantic love and death always appear together. I once asked a class of fifteen-year-old girls to pool all their topics of interest and then rank them in order of priority. They were free to list all imaginable topics. After the results were tabulated, the three main topics were love, death, and sex.

Love and death are closely associated because the intense emotion and transport of being in love usually involve an apparent merging of the lover and beloved to such an extent that a loss of independent identity results. "You're mine" and "I'm yours" have been repeated in love songs a million times over. This is an archetypal inflation. It is the archetypal need to surrender to God, transferred to personal relations. No human being can properly be said to "belong" to another. That would be a form of slavery.

"Dying" is also a common hyperbole of speech that suggests an overwhelming desire. The French speak of "dying" when they have an orgasm. "I'm absolutely dying for a cigarette," the addicted smoker might say. This same hyperbolic figure has sometimes served as a euphemism for romantic love, for the union of two into one flesh radically compromises the separate borders of each person. "My great miseries in this world have been Heathcliffe's miseries," exclaims the elder Catherine in Emily Brontë's scorching novel, *Wuthering Heights*; ". . . my great thought in living is himself. If all else perished, and he remained, I should still continue to be; and if all else remained, and he were annihilated, the universe would turn to a mighty stranger. I should not seem a part of it. . . . I am Heathcliffe!"[4] Romance can be as intoxicating and as addictive as any drug!

As we recall, when the twins parted, they exchanged hearts, and so they were separated not only from each other, but from their selves as well. Their own hearts didn't belong to them any longer. Any person who attempts to live with another's heart, or who gives his own heart away to another, is not himself any longer. He is psychologically "dead" as an individual human being.

A woman with a man's heart has lost her own feminine integrity and has adopted a male version of anima feeling. In this condition, her basic sense is that she belongs to the man, not to her own being. Of course, the equivalent is true for a man who has adopted a woman's heart in place of his own.

In myths and dreams, a death represents the disappearance of a content of consciousness into the unconscious, where it will have immediate contact with the instinctive and archetypal depths of the psyche, there to be transformed and eventually reappear as a new and more vital ingredient of living. This new energy will appear in the child Gregory, as we shall see later.

In the same century in which our tale circulated, there was an explosive development in southwestern Europe involving the birth of a literature of romantic love. Our tale is part of that corpus. In the south of France, poets and traveling minstrels composed ballads of romantic ecstasy. They sang of the image of love personified in a beautiful and gracious lady passing from the eye of her gentleman beholder to his (own!) heart, where true love was felt to be born. This kind of love exemplifies the incestuous "doubling back" of psychological energy that I discussed earlier. It is an introverting of the love interest toward the interior kingdom of the heart. This is symbolic incest.

The new romantic love, sung by the medieval French troubadours and German Minnesingers ("love singers") and first storied by the twelfth-century Provençal court poets, was called *amor*. It was not the *agape*, or spiritual love, taught by the church. Nor was it erotic desire, the instinctive striving of one sexual organ for another. *Amor* was a new kind of love founded upon a conscious appreciation of the *nobility* of nature and the feminine.

Amor started with the senses, where we perceive the outward projections of our inner unconscious complexes and archetypal images, but it did not end there. From the physical eyes of the lover beholding his beloved, this image traveled *inwardly* to the heart (which is located on the left, or "sinister," side of the breast), where love was born from the pleasure that the heart experienced at such a sight.

It was said that amor could only be born in the heart of a person who was "noble-hearted," meaning one who possessed the features of refinement, courtesy, art, temperance, loyalty, and courage. With these qualities the heart could guide the senses to the true realization of love. It is quite apparent that the twin brother was not well endowed with these qualities! His love was too violent, his impulses too primitive, and his heart did not belong sufficiently to himself. Therefore he was incapable of experiencing amor.[5]

The violent form of emotional longing that gripped the twins is not love in the sense of true relatedness, nor does it seem to agree with the definitions of *amor*. It is not the sort of affection upon which any healthy or lasting relationship might be built in the real world. The twins' connection took the form of a compulsive identity of the one with the other. This amounts to a selfish and egotistical confusion of persons. These siblings had been drawn into a symbiotic and displaced experience of a divine archetypal image, so they abused each other and themselves. Today we would call them "codependent." They were playing God to each other. They were possessing and using each other's hearts for selfish purposes. This is the disastrous ecstasy of romance that so many of us crave today. It is our insanity.

Such intense, compulsive, and addictive passion is not uncommon between people who have "fallen in love." It is frequently observed in adolescents, particularly those who are somewhat emotionally unstable. Often the first experience of being in love is so powerful that one partner feels sure he cannot live a day longer without the other close at hand. He feels he *must have* the other person. This is a most blatant form of addiction, not love.

Here is a dream from a woman in her late thirties:

I am participating in an intense and powerful nighttime ritual. I am naked and completely covered by sweat, after vigorous activity like dancing. I am adorned with multiple strands of large wooden and clay beads around my neck. I am menstruating heavily, and the blood issues from my body in strange configurations. In a deep trance state and on the verge of passing out, I drop to my knees on the earth in front of a fire.

A dark-skinned man (Indian or African) approaches me from behind out of the darkness. I cannot see him but I know who he is. He is a beloved to me; I love him intensely and welcome his presence. He touches my temples from behind and suddenly my mind is gone—all sense of ego or self is completely obliterated (however, I am still aware of observing the dream). My consciousness passes instead into the blood that flows from my body; I become one with the blood, I am the blood. Where my mind had been, now a selfless void, my consort's spirit enters. I become filled with his presence and consciousness. He is "in" me as I am "in" the blood, simultaneously. At the same time, the beads around my neck magically come to life and begin to writhe around my neck like snakes (although they are still beads). It is pure ecstasy.

This dream depicts the union of masculine and feminine energies in a most primal way. The heavy flow of menstrual blood suggests the creative force of this woman's personality. In reality she is a talented musician and composer. If this woman were to attempt to live out some version of this dream in relation to an actual man like the one to whom the dream alludes, she would be in a disastrous "in-love" situation comparable to that of the twins in our story. Wisely she kept to an inner experience of this figure. The "pure ecstasy" of the ordeal indicates that the energy of the Self encompasses the dreamer and her consort.

The erotic power of deity swamps all the action of this dream, including the dreamer's ego consciousness. For her mind to pass into the menstrual blood may symbolize that she is totally identified with her archetypal feminine nature but has lost an awareness of who or what she is as an individual feminine human being with a separate life to live in the world.

The writhing snakes of her necklace suggest that she herself, as an ego, is identified with the Great Goddess who is at one with the archetypal depths of the natural psyche. Although this dream hints at the enormous talent and energy that are at this woman's disposal, it could spell trouble if she is not successful in keeping her ordinary ego intact and discriminated from such high-powered and ecstatic energies. I suggested to this woman that she improvise a series of rituals to objectify the symbols in her dream, and demarcate that action in a special area of her life from the ordinary and practical affairs of her daily existence. Perhaps this could be done through her music. This woman needed to authenticate the material of her dream, but at the same time gain some protection from it.

The fact that the twins' inflated and neurotic love for each other could not accomplish the principle of amor helped to foster the "wasteland." The wasteland condition of the realm was the result of the twins' hiding and repressing their sin. They succumbed to the fixed concepts and official patriarchal wisdom of their day. This wisdom dictated that erotic energy must be either channeled into an arranged and loveless marriage or displaced to the ethereal and bloodless spirituality of a jealous patriarchal God. From his omnipotent position, by his monarchical transcendentism and absolutistic moralism, this furious deity "violated" the kingdom of the human heart, the realm of the feminine. Any interior or creative ennoblement of nature or immanent divinity within the psyche—the Divine Child—was taboo. It would give too much credit and value to the feminine, to nature and instinct. In this scheme of things, there was no room for amor, the birth of love within the human heart.

We might say that the jealous suitor who eventually invades the duchess's lands is the brother in a displaced and projected form. Since the brother was banished and died, he has "returned" in the form of a standard marriage candidate for the twin sister. This amounts to an assault upon and an invasion of feminine nature. It is simply another rape! The feminine is becoming a victim of patriarchal violence once again.

In his book *The Masks of God: Creative Mythology*, Joseph Campbell has most impressively characterized the wasteland as "the land where myth is patterned by authority, not emergent from life, where there is no poet's eye to see, no adventure to be lived, where all is set for all and forever . . . a land where poets languish, and priestly spirits thrive, whose task it is to repeat, enforce, and elucidate cliches . . . any world in which force and not love, indoctrination, not education, authority, not experience, prevail in the ordering of lives, and where myths and rites enforced and received are consequently unrelated to the actual inward realizations, needs, and potentialities of those upon whom they are impressed."[6]

Such was the condition of European society and religion in the century in which our tale had its inception. And such were the circumstances of our twins after they naively capitulated to the good advice of their elderly counselor, the purveyor of the standard father-values of the day.

And we, most of us, are sunk in such a dilemma to this very hour. Many of us who can no longer stomach these dried-up clichés have simply abandoned the whole cartload of tradition and wander through life according to random impulse, seeking our artless "kicks" wherever we can find them.

SIX

THE NIGHT-SEA
JOURNEY

At about the same time that the duchess learns of her dear brother's tragic death, two peasant fishermen are struggling with their tackle one morning as their boat lurches and tosses upon the swells of an abating storm near their island community.

Suddenly they catch sight of a little skiff riding in the heavy surf. It appears to be empty. But as they reach it, they discover that it in fact contains a small chest securely tied inside.

As they bring their mysterious cargo to shore, they are met by their superior, Gregory, the ruling abbot of the local community. In his presence they open the chest and, to their wonder and amazement, find an infant boy, alive and healthy, though not quite dry. He is carefully wrapped in the most exquisite silk brocade fabric. At his feet lies a remarkable ivory tablet encrusted with jewels, and scattered around him in the chest is a fortune in gold coins!

An episode of abandonment to the dark ocean waves followed by a miraculous survival is a well-known theme in the history of the world's folklore. The great German ethnologist Leo Frobenius termed it the *night-sea journey*.[1]

In the night-sea journey the hero travels an adventurous dark water journey through the underworld and generally ends up as a prize-winner, bringing a new experience or value to life. For this reason the hero is likened mythically to the sun, which every night makes its perilous journey into darkness below the horizon and reemerges, triumphant, with the dawn.

Often this underworld night-sea is conceived of as a demonic ogress or monster-dragon who swallows the hero and attempts to keep him within her belly, which becomes a kind of "womb-tomb." Usually, however, this prodigious fellow finds a means of escape, which generally depends upon his courage, skill, and resourcefulness, as well as a little magic in his favor.

Psychologically, this solar hero works within, bringing us a whole new lease on life and a new attitude toward our experience. He goes to hell and back, and this is our inner experience of getting a powerful new bearing on life. He is at once the Wise Old Man and the Divine Child. He is tradition, and at the same time a revelation of the most up-to-date wisdom. He is the consciousness that sheds new light on our existence, redeeming our wholeness. With his help we gain a vital new awareness to "fathom" a mood or a disconcerting confusion or pressure in our thoughts and arrive at a new and better attitude for living.

Whether we are men or women trying to come to terms with troublesome thoughts, moods, obsessions, or compulsive behavior, we must find a way of entering into the territory of our difficulties without being *possessed* by them. The solar hero conquering the darkness is a new consciousness that has risen out of a meeting with the dark side of our own nature, but has not succumbed to or been seduced by the raw impulses or emotions that captivate our awareness out of the abyss of the unconscious psyche.

When a man is gripped by a mood, he is in the belly of the night-sea monster. She contains and entraps him. That is, his mood is all around him. Everything—other people, the weather, the vicissitudes of his career, even the color of the wallpaper— seems to reflect it.

He stubs his toe getting out of bed. He can't find any sharp razor blades. "Somebody" used up all the hot water for his shower. Predictably, the family washing machine has once again digested four socks, but no two from the same pairs. The eggs aren't cooked right and the coffee tastes awful. "As usual" the children are fighting. His wife seems casual, distracted, indifferent, even flippant. Everything he encounters is obviously irritating, depressing, ugly, or just plain wrong, and he with it! It is as if "fate" had made it that way, and it doesn't appear that he can do anything about it. He'd like to tell the whole world to go to hell, and then maybe bust a few heads just for the fun of it. He has been transformed into an irritated and grouchy old bear.

In this circumstance, a man would do well to stop for a moment and say to himself out loud, "I am very strong and clever. Let me plant my feet firmly! Let me stay wide awake now. Exactly what am I experiencing? What does my awful mood look like to me? Can I picture it to myself in images? Precisely how do I feel about it? What would it say if it could talk to me?" Then something very miraculous may happen. The man will still encounter his difficulties, but in a very different way. He will have his mood as a feeling attitude *within* his male consciousness. His feminine mood will not totally imprison all his male consciousness within her dark belly of hell. The man will no longer be *possessed* by his mood. A major revelation will have occurred and a new attitude formed. Of course this sounds quite simple and easy. In practice it is far more difficult. Possession by an unconscious complex gives the ego a feeling of righteous and grandiose certainty. Under such circumstances, reflective self-criticism or insight seems completely unnecessary and will be vehemently rejected if its need is suggested.

Men are seduced by unconscious feelings that appear most often as an illusory atmosphere enveloping their lives. Women are intruded upon by autonomous and primitively unconscious thoughts that seem more like preconceived opinions than active analyses or conscious assessments. These anima and animus possessions are the little insanities in our daily lives.

Because women are dominantly feminine, they do not fall into the belly of the monster in so direct a fashion. It is the state of their minds, or their autonomous thought patterns, which are swallowed up by the abyss and therefore become so dark, depressing, confusing, prejudiced, and unilluminating to them. "I can't get my hair to do what I want it to!" "I feel fat and ugly!" "I must seem so boring to other people. No man will ever be interested in me, now that I'm over forty. My breasts are beginning to sag!" "He glared at me this morning. Maybe I deserved it. I wish I could tell him how to help me have an orgasm but I'm worried he'll get insulted and turned off." "None of my clothes look right on me." "I feel so guilty about my children, leaving them all day long the way I do. What a terrible mother I am!" "Maybe nothing will ever change—I guess I'm doomed. Nothing I plan ever works. I try to be aggressive, but I always make a damn fool of myself." "I'm a complete mess as a person!"

In a certain sense, a woman's deeper femininity *is* the night-sea monster, though it is much more positive in her than in most men. Therefore, if she will only wake up to herself and say, "What are these dark thoughts and depressing opinions that are passing through me and seem to possess me? As a woman, I am bigger than they are. My big womb-psyche can contain them all. I'm not afraid of them. I was here before they arrived, and I shall survive after they are gone. So what do I have to be afraid of? Let me see how *I* feel about them, and also what *I* think of them, for I have my *own* thoughts!" Then this hellish underworld may be transformed into an experience of new life, a kind of Garden of Eden for this woman. Then her feminine strength will blossom. Her passivity to unconscious prejudice will be changed to deliberately conscious thinking and feeling.

This is how we take responsibility for our psychological difficulties and act as the "re-creators" of our selves—how we "be-
get" ourselves. When we feel "terrible," we are in the underworld
abyss, overwhelmed and flooded by the unconscious psyche. But
the old myths remind us that the darkness of depression,
faithlessness, and feeling "dead" contains a secret promise if we
can only maintain our balance and our conscious integrity. There
is indeed a light at the end of the tunnel when we feel ourselves to
be in "the shadow of death."

This means that if we can keep our egos a bit to one side, then
our conscious mental attitudes can be changed and revitalized
through their own demise. Often we must "give up" and "let go" in
order to "let God"![2] Such a cycle is built into our psychology and
will come to our aid if we can only recognize it and "go with it."
We are desperately in need of this inner solar hero quality in our
lives today. It is important to realize that our ego is not the hero
himself. That hero is something transpersonal within us, which
can recycle our attitudes and outlook on living. It is precisely he
who can survive and solve our depressiveness and our faithlessness. This inner archetypal hero-child is the modern psychological equivalent of the old incestuous celestial deity. To be realized
and appreciated, he requires a goddess-vessel, that is, an interior sense of soul or psyche, where the actual spiritual events of
one's life are experienced.

Though many men may appear strong and confident on the
outside, inside it is a different matter. Much of the apparent
"macho" behavior of men is a compensation for an inward sensitivity and fear of the power of the feminine goddess. A man's
mood is more threatening and overpowering to him inwardly than
any outward challenge by the most virulent male aggressor. It
strikes him where he is the most defenseless, from inside his own
soul. Men are "castrated" in the stability and reality of their
consciousness every day when they are seized by a mood.

Oftentimes men carefully regulate their accessibility to the
world of "emotions" by refusing to acknowledge this realm
of experience. They stay safely in their "heads" and occupy

themselves with "plain logic," "hard facts," and "concrete reality." This gives them a certain protection from the anima side of life, but it amounts to an enormous sacrifice. Whenever a situation arises that requires a feminine touch, like insight into another person's feelings or his own, such a man is at a complete loss. All he can do is try to "fix things up" by instituting a new program, or by making continual suggestions and then getting upset when they are not followed, or simply by reinforcing discipline and authority. Usually he just gets angry and frustrated or depressed and blames somebody, as if that will solve the problem.

Some problems in life simply require love, presence, and simple human acknowledgment for their solution, but many men are frightened to death of entering such a murky territory, for fear they will lose their way. Men automatically assume they have to do something, rather than appreciate, share with, or be with a person who has a problem. Men often mistakenly interpret receptiveness, openness, or relatability as being passive. Some modern "liberated" women do this too.

Whenever a man has to do with feelings, then immediately the image of a "devouring mother" comes up. It takes a real heroic confidence and trust in himself for a man to encounter his own feelings or those of a woman consciously and learn something from the experience. This is real masculinity, not macho posturing. If a man could just sit down for a few minutes each day and carefully acknowledge and study his feelings, or those of his wife, without prejudice, his awareness and general vitality and perspective on life would be enormously expanded.

Most men fail at this because they have a lot of trouble focusing on feelings, which to them are like intangible and fleeting vapors, about which they have great trouble speaking or making any concrete sense. If you ask a man what his feelings are, he will probably tell you all his logical thoughts on the subject. He doesn't quite realize how he is systematically distancing himself from his feelings because of his fear of the unknown and the unfamiliar. Inside he is petrified of the dark abyss in his psyche. But he can take heart.

In our tale, the infant boy has been abandoned to the sea. This new life, the twins' son, was the product of their incest. He takes on the hero role in which his father failed, and travels on the archetypal journey through the underworld, survives the ordeal, and is rescued safely. This little fellow is the "new day" of European culture, which each of us is struggling consciously or unconsciously to realize in our modern souls. He represents a new form of consciousness that results from a union of masculine and feminine principles on an equal par with each other. It is almost as if the heart and the mind had joined together to produce something new and unique in the world, not from the adjustment-requirements of the surrounding patriarchal culture, but from the actual needs and potentialities of the deep soul.

Something like this has never happened on a large scale before in the entire history of the world. It is a uniquely modern phenomenon. It is a flourishing growth from seeds originally planted in the twelfth century. What happened mythologically in this medieval tale is now struggling to take place in our experience of living. Our little hero is the Self-realization of our modern individual consciousness.

In our tale, the father-duke's old advisor encourages the twins to cover up what has happened, in order to protect the security of the realm and avoid scandal. But the incest between the twins is a symptom of the need for renewal. The little son of the twins is the nascent beginning of this new consciousness.

Symbolically, the "incest" is a turning of attention and value away from the outer and "normal" world of official collective consciousness toward the unconscious depths. Not only does such a revolt threaten the security and stability of standard programs of living, but, more important, it runs the risk of dissolving ego consciousness altogether and bringing about irresponsible infantility or even insanity. Fears about such an eventuality are not entirely unfounded. Numerous myths the world over describe failed heroes or maverick adventurers who stumble into the forbidden realm, never to be seen again. The Great Mother unconscious simply eats them alive.

Real individuation that achieves a deep transformation of the psyche requires immense courage and tenacity, enormous ego strength, and a sufficient capacity for sustained responsibility. Much is at stake in the hero journey. It is a struggle that can be lost.

It is not sufficient merely to "drop out" of the bottom of the collectively conscious world and enter upon a mystic or exotic journey into the hinterlands of the psyche. That is not even so hard to do, if one has a penchant for such things. One of the real challenges is to keep some means of connection, some "Ariadne's thread" in order to find one's way back again, and then actually go through to the end of the journey. Otherwise it is only craziness and a disastrous confusion.

Just such a thread is our sense of responsible guilt. For the pang of guilt tells us just where and how we have departed from cultural conventions. True responsibility and accountability (not a guilt-ridden mood) that are consciously acknowledged and valued keep our consciousness intact and at the same time allow us to be aware of the precise nature of our transgression. In religious language one might say that the consciousness of sin is the pathway to God. The Apostle Paul was even moved to ask whether we should not remain in sin in order that the grace of God might have greater scope.[3]

Morality ought not to be a form of brainwashing or repression, but a force for the raising of new and individual consciousness. If a child is punished but also forgiven for playing with the control knobs on the kitchen gas stove, he will be reminded of his curiosity. He will be more conscious, and also more in charge of his impulses to explore the environment. Such discipline will reinforce his self-knowledge, and his appetite for new horizons.

Our English word *pardon* comes from the Latin *per*, "thoroughly," and *donare*, "to give," in other words, "to give thoroughly." A firm but loving pardon, mediated by a parent, counselor, friend, or minister of God, does not annihilate the wrongdoing. It is not a "cover-up." Rather, it reinforces and reminds us of our ambivalent predicament, where certain impulses, ideas, or feelings have risen up in contradiction to the acceptable norm. Pardoning or forgiveness discriminates the unconscious expression of one's impulses from a healthy appreciation of instinct. This builds a reflective self-awareness. A pardon gives us back thoroughly to our whole selves. The careful understanding and loving discipline of a child, or of our own selves when we are older, breeds both competent adjustment to society *and* awareness of innovative and potentially creative capacities. In this way a critical and active adjustment is made ideally to the inner and the outer worlds at the same time. Such is the task of the tiny foundling now safely in the abbot's hands.

The mythic scheme of this solar night-sea odyssey is that when the sun has finally come to its setting in the evening, the sun-hero dies and at the same time impregnates the mother-ogress as he enters her underworld belly. Falling asleep, dying, being eaten, and sexual union with impregnation are all the same thing in this mythic moment.

The night-sea journey itself is both a devouring imprisonment and a gestation of the new fetal sun-god, who is destined to succeed his late father. With the approach of the succeeding dawn, this rejuvenated celestial deity miraculously escapes his gestational womb-tomb-prison and rises invincibly from the eastern horizon to rule the new day. In this manner he is seen to have conquered darkness and death. In such a context one is reminded of the Christian version of this mythologem, superbly rendered in lines attributed to Saint Francis of Assisi: "Dying we live, and are reborn through death's dark night to endless day."[4]

In this mythic system the masculine heroic figure alternates constantly between father and son. As father he grows old and dies. As son he is eternally begotten as young and new. Like a seed-corpse buried in the field of Mother Earth, his body in death is synonymously an impregnation of the goddess' womb. The following day, the erstwhile god is regenerated in the form of his own child, and the process starts all over again.

The feminine night-ocean is at once the dark virgin-bride of god and the mother of this same solar deity, wherein the father and the son are of "one substance" though of differing "persons" in the eternal seasons of life and death. Participating with full awareness in this archetypal drama is the means by which we may act as the regenerators of our own lives. Much of Christian dogma is directed toward these universal psychological facts.

Jung saw such mythic themes of ever-cycling death and resurrection as indications of how consciousness changes or "transforms" from one period of culture to another, and from one stage of psychological development to the next in a single human lifetime. For Jung, these myths are outward projections of innate inner psychological energy states, part of the basic structure of the objective psyche.[5]

This dynamic symbolic process begins by leading consciousness back ("regressing" it) toward its childlike condition in the unconscious. "Except a man be born again, he cannot see the Kingdom of Heaven."[6] In the Christian version of renewal, the sacrament of baptism, this regeneration is symbolized by water and the idea of an invisible Spirit. Such a rebirth is, of course, not literal or physical but psychological. The water of baptism represents a symbolic amniotic fluid, a variant expression of the night-sea ocean just described. It refers not to the womb of our personal mother, but to the uterus of Life itself, to the creative feminine principle. In its traditional Latin rite for the blessing of the baptismal font on the Saturday before Easter, the Roman Catholic liturgy speaks of the font to which we return as the *uterus ecclesiae*, the "womb of the church."

We humans must experience spiritual transformation or our vulgar existence will become a living death. For a sacramental rite to be effective, it cannot remain simply on the level of blind faith, credal belief, or mere ecclesiastical polity. Its symbols must actually effect a psychological change by leading the libido, or psychic energy, back into the unconscious on a hero journey toward the depths of the personality. If many of these traditional rites and rituals no longer seem to have an overwhelming and effective impact on the psyche, at least they give us a strong hint about what is required somewhere somehow. Today, we desperately need a new access to this deep source of transformation.

Our little mariner in his chest has traveled in a second womb. When he is fished out of the ocean, therefore, he is "twice-born." It is this second birth that moves the boy beyond the psychology of his parents and their narrow cultural attitudes to a new possibility of authentic consciousness.

It is as if another, far greater life had taken possession of him. His life is destined to drop out of the ethnic and the personal into the universal and the mythic.

The great archetypal wheel of psychological transformation has begun to turn once more, and the little hero-captain is now its chief player in the dramatic action.

SEVEN

◆

THE SHADOW OF PERFECTION

AFTER the fishermen have opened the chest and discovered the child, Abbot Gregory quickly scans the ornate ivory tablet, and then, taking note of the twenty gold marks and the precious silk, he acts quickly.

To one of the fishermen he gives two gold marks, persuading him to take the child home to his wife to rear until it has grown old enough to enter the monastery school. He gives another gold coin to the second fisherman, charging both men to keep the child's unusual discovery a strict secret. Seventeen gold coins remain.

The first fisherman is instructed to tell people that he and his wife are raising his brother's daughter's child, his own grand-nephew. The abbot then instructs the new stepfather to appear within a few days at the gate of the monastery and make a formal request to have the child baptized.

Shortly afterward this is all accomplished. At the ceremony in the monastery chapel, the abbot himself acts as both the god-father and the administrant of the sacrament. He gives this exquisite child his own name: Gregory.

The rich silks are carefully put away, and the remaining seventeen gold marks are shrewdly invested through a Jewish banker known to the community. The tablet itself, with its disquieting inscription, is deposited in the abbot's private chamber, safe from all prying eyes.

Young Gregory is raised in the peasant fisherman's family until he reaches six years of age. Then he is taken into the monastery school. There he quickly proves to be a highly competent scholar in every course of study. His demeanor is always gracious and correct, and he ignores nothing that might lead him to honor and decency.

He is as perfect as any child could be. Gregory possesses whatever it is that earns praise and commendation on this earth. As he grows older, he asks questions of every kind. By the time he has reached his early teens, his mental life has become almost sagelike. In grammar, divinity, theology, and the law, he excels above all his peers.

Meanwhile, year after year, the fisherman's wife, whose existence has been considerably improved by the gift of the two gold marks, ever and again prods her husband to tell her where the child really came from. The fisherman repeatedly refuses to divulge this secret. But finally, after incessant pestering, he reveals to his wife that Gregory is in fact a foundling, whom they had pulled out of the frothy sea. But his wife obediently honors her husband's decree that this be kept completely private.

Now, although Gregory is well along in his studies at the monastery school, he still enjoys the companionship of his illiterate peasant stepbrothers, whom he considers to be his cousins.

One day, as Gregory roughhouses with one of these boys about his own age, he suddenly lands a powerful blow to the other's face, badly hurting him. The injured boy runs home screaming to his mother that Gregory has struck him on purpose! Gregory has followed the boy and is hiding just outside the door of their cottage. He hears the heated exchange that takes place between mother and son.

Within seconds, this peasant mother explodes into anger and rage. She shouts at the top of her lungs that Gregory is certainly no child of hers, but instead a miserable foundling, a "nobody" who was dragged out of the sea by the fishermen years ago! No, she won't for a minute stand for his beating up on her own dear boy! Who is he to do that? Nobody even knows who he is or where he comes from. He is an alien stranger, a castaway! He is no relation to any of them at all, certainly no cousin. That was just a silly tale they had told.

When Gregory hears this, a lightning shock streaks through him. He can hardly believe his ears. What to do? Immediately he runs back to the monastery to tell the abbot what has happened and all that he has heard from his stepmother's very own lips. On the way, the thought grows in his mind that he must leave this island and roam the world. He belongs nowhere, to no one.

Gregory, the decent, intelligent, and perfect child, has suddenly experienced a rude awakening.

In the Middle Ages, a child with no legitimate parents, no inherited slot in the family or community, was considered a derelict, almost a pariah, the meanest and lowliest of all creatures. Abandoned children or foundlings were thought to be in the same class with murderers, thieves, jugglers, and strolling louts. Not to have blood relations was almost a crime in itself.[1]

What does this sudden revelation mean psychologically? Gregory went to school and from the beginning modeled his behavior and values on the best examples known to him, which were informed by the civilized Christian ideals of gentleness, intelligence, rationality, and nobility of spirit. Though brilliant, he was a docile and malleable subject in the hands of his tutors and superiors. He was well on his way to becoming the perfect specimen.

Something rather analogous happens today when children are

disciplined by their parents and teachers to behave appropriately, follow the rules, think before they act, strive for excellence in their studies, use good manners, and be sensitive and considerate toward others.

But this rigorous training of the outward persona and the rational mind does not touch every aspect or level of the personality. Certain parts of the human constitution are unable or unwilling to comply with the strict requirements of such a dutiful and civilized program. And to complicate matters even more, we aren't even doing a very good job nowadays in training the persona traits of children. This stems from our ambivalence and vagueness about our role as parents and our refusal or inability to structure our children's lives with authority.

Be that as it may, the deeper instinctive psyche not only remains relatively untouched by such training, but reacts negatively to it. This darker, interior side of the psyche, which is not so fond of being goaded into perfection, Jung called the shadow.

Being too one-sidedly "good" forces a repression and a devaluing of the impulsive and instinctive part of the psyche. Thus a gulf or split widens that cripples the capacity for natural and spontaneous living. In addition, enormous energy is required to maintain this awkward system of imbalance, which deprives consciousness of a basic resource.

Ironically, a relatively severe moral and social indoctrination, with the devaluing and systematic repression of instinctive behavior that such a program entails, is absolutely necessary if a rudimentary consciousness and suitable persona are ever to be gained in the first place. Otherwise children would remain relatively unconscious, primitive, irresponsible, and unadapted to the needs of society. This is the tragic price we pay for civilization.

Nevertheless, whenever an exclusively coherent moral and ethical attitude is formed in consciousness, there arises in the unconscious a compensatory opposite polarity, consisting of all the psychic elements that are left out of this established conscious attitude, because they are incompatible with it. The Devil always gets his due.

If we try very hard to be pure, honorable, selfless, and good, then the counterpole in the unconscious will be a shady opportunist who prowls around the back streets of our heart and mind in search of what he can get for himself any way he can, even to the point of committing criminal or sadistic violence. This "shadow" is simply the other side of the ideal attitude. It reacts to any very extreme or narrow development of ego consciousness that ignores the needs of wholeness for the sake of "right living." Probably the most famous literary example of this split from the dark side is Robert Louis Stevenson's *Dr. Jekyll and Mr. Hyde.* What is particularly interesting about this tale is that the whole story came originally from one of Stevenson's dreams.

But the first experiences of the shadow are never those which involve direct insight into one's own character. The first encounters with this dark inner brother or sister usually take the form of victimization by unconscious impulses that get out of control and projections of this dark side onto other persons of the same sex. We are far more likely to take it out on our neighbor, or on someone whom we accuse to be the culprit, than we are to look within ourselves to find out what we are really struggling against.

For the brilliant and perfect boy to strike his peasant brother with no apparent provocation suggests that Gregory has displaced his own inner conflict onto his relations with his stepbrother. He must have unconsciously had his nose in the air and partly contributed to whatever the problem was between them.

The "hostile brothers" is a well-known theme from folklore and mythology. In the ancient Egyptian tale, Set murdered his brother Osiris. By a ruse, he got Osiris to lie down in a coffin. Set slammed the cover on and nailed it tightly shut, then dumped it into the Nile River, where it floated down to the sea (another instance of the "night-sea" journey).

In the biblical tale of Cain and Abel, each brother brought the product of his labor as a gift to God. Cain, the gardener, offered various fruits and vegetables. Abel, the herdsman, presented some of his animals as a gift. God looked with favor on Abel's offering, and spurned Cain's, so Cain murdered his brother.[2]

The hostile brothers represent the typical conflict of good and evil as opposites, which arises whenever an exclusive and one-sided point of view is established in consciousness. In the biblical story, God accepted Abel's sheep and rejected Cain's produce. This is precisely the way conscious attitudes and values are often formed, quite arbitrarily, with no appreciation of wholeness or psychological balance. In the same way, Gregory became the perfect specimen of the up and coming learned monk, but how one-sided it was! Then everything fell apart.

When Gregory strikes an intense blow to his brother, this represents a last straw for the shadow, who finally reacts. We are constantly mistreating our shadow selves, insisting on one sort of perfection or another, and it usually has something to do with an impeccable self-image or persona.

We generally have rather strict and ideal requirements in mind and seldom allow much consideration for that side of ourselves which springs more from nature and instinct than from the need to perform and conform. This other, apparently "inferior" side has its own needs, requirements, and agenda, which are necessary for our health and well-being. We would do well to make our peace with this part, not by giving in to crudely impulsive and primitive-emotional behavior, but by consciously and deliberately giving up our inflated insistence on being so perfect and honorable. Such perfectionism itself springs from the childish need to please authority figures whom we either fear or admire. We want desperately to belong and fit in with a collective type of self-respect in society.

But from the shadow's point of view, "good behavior" seems to be a form of cruelest punishment, and a heavy price is paid within ourselves. Our dreams usually tell us all. A young white man dreamed early in his analysis:

I parked my car at the edge of Harlem near the Hudson River, and I was very much looking forward to eating at a certain restaurant on the East Side, but it was made known to me that I would be required to walk through the entire breadth of these tenement neighborhoods, through poverty and squalor, and to experience it all firsthand and face up to it! Then I would be allowed to dine at the restaurant.

At one point I found myself in a dark, dank, and foul-smelling subway station. Way off to one side, in an abandoned underground hallway, I saw an old and indigent black man, sick and probably dying. He was lying in a pile of garbage and urine and was futilely trying to swallow a dirty scrap of paper with the word *sandwich* scrawled upon it. I found this poor man's situation so pathetic and disgusting that I broke down in tears. "What have we done to these people?" I thought.

After I had been exposed to innumerable scenes of this kind, only then was I allowed to continue on to the restaurant. It was a wonder I had any appetite left. I'm not sure if I ever got to the restaurant.

Such a dream shows the condition of a whole aspect of this man's personality, the shadow side, that was being given only casual lip-service but no real care or psychological nourishment. Within the depths of this man's psyche was a veritable ghetto of forgotten and starving humanity. But on the conscious surface he was a "good" person. Despite his good intentions outwardly, he was neglecting a large part of his instinctual self, which was barely surviving.

In our modern and more socially conscious world, we have made some strides in recognizing the great harm produced by racial prejudice and economic exploitation. Yet such a dream shows that the very same injustice exists also on the *inside* of the white man. How can the white man help his black brother in the human community when he is riddled with the very same problem inside himself? How can he appreciate injustice, brutality, and desperate need on the outside if the thing itself runs rampant in his own soul? One hopes the dreamer could never be the same person after such an experience.

In our tale, when the peasant mother sides with the shadow stepbrother and reveals Gregory's questionable origin, we might say that in the unconscious a sort of "Mother-Nature" figure begins to shift the balance away from favoring the conscious and more civilized point of view, in order that nature and instinct may have a chance. In so doing, the well-ordered and esteemed conscious program is completely upset. Gregory's life is irrevocably changed. He may no longer remain in the comfortable monastery school, enjoying the immense admiration of his peers and superiors. He has suddenly gone from top to bottom, which constitutes a total reversal of values, what Jung called by the Greek term *enantiodromia*, which means "to go around the other way."³

Young Gregory had been working against instinct toward a more civilized and cultivated personality. Then an aggressive impulse suddenly reared its ugly head, in obvious contrast to his gentle and intelligent nature.

Jung observed that God has a funny way of periodically dropping us on our heads for no apparent reason!

Our tale condenses into one startling episode an event that happens repeatedly in the lives of young people as they grow toward adulthood under the supervision of parents and teachers. Every time a child is reprimanded for a violation of the code and suffers the bite of shame, there is occasion for alienation. Being sent to one's room, having a favorite pastime prohibited, or having certain plans canceled as a punishment brings on a sense of rejection and negative judgment. The child is no longer bathed in the easy glow of comfortable approval in a family atmosphere where his or her self-esteem may be taken for granted. Especially to a sensitive child, such a show of disapproval is a terrible slap in the face, and the sense of shame cuts deeply into the child's sense of adequacy and emotional security. Some parents, having reached the limit of their tolerance, may even exclaim, "I don't know where you came from!"

In some young people this split takes the form of a nagging feeling that they simply don't fit in. "I just don't belong!" "I'm different." "No one understands me!" "I feel weird, like a stranger among my friends." "My family and I don't seem to have *anything* in common."

This loss of easy collective approval, whether it stems from an outward collision with authority, with peers, or from within as a nagging doubt about one's sense of belonging, heralds a big change in consciousness that is like a fall from grace. Feelings of doubt, fear, and pain replace the idyllic and innocent pleasure of always being a good child and getting rewarded for it.

Today, not a few children grow up with hardly any experience of this biting rejection. These are the "normal" children of our culture. The way of adventurous searching on the path to enlightenment is probably closed to them. In their own way, they have enough to satisfy themselves already. They are reasonably successful and well adjusted. The psychology of the saint or the sage is not relevant to their lives. Only those children who suffer severe pain and deprivation at some level in their experience will ever grow to become truly exceptional. A normal child has no good reason to transcend his culture or grow beyond it. Ironically, most healthy and well-adjusted children grow up to be relatively prosaic adults.

Gregory learns that he is a foundling, that he is literally different, with entirely other origins, a boy who is "out of it" as far as the local culture is concerned. Also, in learning that he was abandoned to the sea, he realizes that for some reason his parents didn't want him. This is probably the worst news of all. He was unwanted, unloved, perhaps even hated, else why did they give him up to the sea, to a virtually certain death?

This inner conflict is the first step in a young person's finding his unique identity and deeper personality. Living under the protection and tutelage of parents and later of their surrogates in the wider culture may be, in the larger scope of things, only a provisional stage of development. It is psychologically possible to move beyond this level of awareness.

Just when does that potentially special and unique person begin to make his appearance? When does one's native disposition begin to develop beyond the confines of the well-adjusted specimen? When does one stop being the "right sort of person" and become the actual person that one is destined to be? When and how does one find one's own genuine self?

This next very special stage of development is rather uncommon or unusual in any marked degree in our mass society. Most people want to belong and fit in, and thereby achieve a relevant status among their conforming peers. It is frightening to be so different. How much authenticity and originality can a "normal" person withstand? Very, very little, apparently.

The inner foundling or orphan is that part of our psyche which is still faithfully attached to the archetypal structures and therefore does not in the least belong to the family or the culture that molded our collective consciousness. It is more than simply a shadow aspect, but is the condition in which we often first encounter the Divine Child, the promise and the potential for all our future development that leads beyond normal adjustment. As Wordsworth has reminded us in his "Intimations of Immortality":[4]

> The soul that rises with us, our life's star,
> Hath had elsewhere its setting,
> And cometh from afar . . .

Theological language says that this interior or essential core of the personality is not the product of human social structures, values, or institutions, but comes from God. This is the deep source of any man's or woman's sense of vocation.

Basically, our tale is telling us how to get back to the basic and whole personality with full consciousness of it. According to the story, one step in such a process is the necessity of being jarred out of one's well-adjusted and respectable (and sometimes depreciated) position in the world, and for a huge question mark to arise as to precisely who and what one is.

The nineteenth-century Hindu sage Sri Ramakrishna told a delightfully charming story to make this very point, concerning such a shift of identity:

> Some people think that they are bound . . . , that they will never attain to Divine Wisdom, or to Divine Love. But all this fear vanishes from the heart of a true disciple if his Guru, or spiritual guide, be gracious to him. There was a flock of sheep in the woods; suddenly a tigress jumped into their midst. At that moment she gave birth to a cub and died on the spot. The kind-hearted sheep took care of the cub, and brought it up among them. They ate grass, the cub followed their example; they bleated, the cub also learned to bleat. In this manner the cub grew up not as a young tiger but like a sheep. One day a full-grown tiger came that way and watched with wonder the grass-eating tiger. The real tiger drew nearer, but the cub began to bleat. Then the real tiger dragged him to the edge of a lake and said: "Look here! Compare your face with mine. Is there any difference? You are a tiger like me; grass is not your food; your food is animal flesh." But the grass-eating tiger could not believe it. After a long time the real tiger convinced him that he was of the same species. Then he gave him a piece of flesh to eat, but he would not touch it; he began once more to bleat and to seek for grass. At last, however, the real tiger forced him to eat animal flesh; at once he liked the taste of the blood, gave up his grass-eating and bleating, and realized that he was not a sheep but a tiger. He then followed the real tiger and became like him. [5]

In our tale, Gregory is passing through an analogous transformation as life itself is grimly initiating him into the knowledge of his own true nature, which is not ultimately comprehended or appreciated by the people of the island community. Like all births, it is frightening and painful, and a kind of awakening from sleep.

We ought not to pass on before we touch briefly upon a major implicating theme of Gregory's sudden shock. The mother's insatiable curiosity about Gregory's origin is certainly critical to the outcome.

The theme of the snoopy and inordinately inquisitive female is scattered through all the pages of folklore and myth. Usually a major disaster results from such tenacious curiosity, which often ends a previous period of unusual happiness and bliss.

Such a relentless inquiry is in fact an inborn impulse within human nature for more consciousness. Though consciousness itself, in both men and women, seems to have a symbolically masculine character, it is invariably a response to a *feminine question*. The feminine and sometimes woman herself seem to present us with life's *enigma*, which man is challenged and often goaded into answering, not always, however, according to his smug expectations. The blissful reputation of ignorance is not entirely beside the mark. Ironically, such utter happiness is usually a symptom that further development is just around the corner, like the fearsome tiger-mentor of Ramakrishna's story. Are not our lives, practically speaking, made up of a series of exploded paradises?

In our tale, Gregory is not this peasant woman's own child. Her husband had ordered her to serve as mother to him. But one suspects that there is a very special mother-son bond between this woman and her own illiterate natural son, which has always rendered Gregory an outsider. And because Gregory was the godson of the abbot-nobleman of the community, he was increasingly the recipient of advantages and prerogatives that were denied this woman's own rustic and unlearned children.

Gregory was the adopted son of the abbot, and therefore the son of another mother, the medieval Catholic Church. In its school Gregory was being educated and "raised" in his consciousness above the more natural state of relatively instinctual peasanthood. He was steadily becoming a more rarefied and more "spiritual" human being and entering another world of intellect, moral reflection, culture, refinement, and taste, a vastly more civilized condition than any peasant boy might normally enjoy. He was steadily "putting on the new man."[6]

Considering all this, we might speculate that the peasant mother, with her more instinctive and impulsive disposition, is a spokesperson for nature itself in the psyche, who is jealous of her own, and is resentful of the violation of the native personality by the patriarchal spiritual force of Christian civilization, which, from the perspective of the twelfth century, had arrived in Europe somewhat recently. In short, she was reacting to the intrusive distortion of instinctive wholeness by the spiritually elitist intellectual and moral influence of the Church.

Gregory, for his part, is getting the first painfully subliminal hint of his underlying and essential tiger quality, and it will now be increasingly difficult for him to live among the sheep.

EIGHT

THE WINDS'
DESIGN

GREGORY immediately runs to the abbot and tells him that he
has just discovered that he, Gregory, is actually a wretched
outcast. Gregory exclaims he must leave immediately and from
now on live the life of a homeless servant. He can't stand the
thought of the shame and the mockery that will certainly come
his way when everybody realizes that he is simply a miserable
foundling, a nobody.

The abbot tries to convince Gregory that everyone loves and
respects him and that he has made a great start in the religious
life. The abbot confides it has always been his hope that Gregory
might one day succeed him as the ruling abbot of the island
community. But Gregory says that he can't stay and divulges that
all his life he has really wanted to be a knight and go on a worldly
quest. He then speaks to the abbot at length of his enthusiasm. In
much colorful detail he describes his fascination for horseman-

ship and how he will ride so magnificently that it will look as if he were virtually "painted onto the horse!"

Gregory goes on to exclaim that he has always longed more for the spear than for the stylus, and that a sword is more dear to him than any pen could be.

Finally the abbot consents, but warns that Gregory cannot get far as a knight because he has no means. Gregory replies that he will earn his way as he goes, by bravery, resoluteness, and valor. He is determined.

Then the abbot produces the rich silk brocade fabric that had been wrapped round Gregory when the fishermen found him in the chest. An order is placed for a patrician suit of clothing to be made from this material. The abbot, as the empowered nobleman of the island, ceremonially dubs Gregory a knight. But then strongly urges Gregory to remain in the territory and be wedded to a young lady of good station and means, so that he will be materially secure. Gregory refuses the abbot's offer, however, insisting that knight-errantry is the only life for him.

Next, the abbot shows Gregory the ivory tablet and the gold. As Gregory reads the tablet, he is devastated. He weeps bitterly and laments his sinful origin. He feels guilty about the secret deed of his parents, even though he himself has done no wrong. But his sadness and grief are relieved by the knowledge that he is a youth of high pedigree, born into a noble family. The abbot still attempts to dissuade Gregory from pursuing knighthood. He warns that in such a life he will expose himself to many occasions for sinning. "Remain," pleads the kindly old monk, "and give over the brief time you have on earth for Life Eternal!"

But Gregory is relentless and states that his desire grows ever more intense for this world and that he wishes to go on an errant quest, "until the grace of God shows me who I am and from whence I came."

The remaining seventeen gold marks, having been well invested, have now grown to one hundred and fifty, and some of this is used to provide Gregory with a sufficient vessel and crew, several warhorses, and equipment and supplies for a voyage.

When it comes time to depart, the abbot accompanies Gregory down to the shore. As Gregory's ship sails away, the two of them, the youth and the old cleric, gaze at each other steadfastly, until the sea broadens between them and they fade from each other's sight.

Immediately, Gregory kneels and prays to God for direction and aid. He tells the helmsman to steer blindly, allowing the ship to go wherever the sea and winds take it. A strong gale blows up. After three days Gregory and his crew are driven near the coast of a strange new land.

So our young Gregory, just passing into midadolescence, is beginning to feel his oats. After his barnyard battle, he has suddenly been imagining himself a knightly horseman, a "chevalier," riding his horse as if he were literally fused with it.

The psychological symbolism of the horse and rider combined is a most interesting one. The horse represents the animal-impulsive side of the unconscious personality, which serves as a foundation for the higher and more conscious power of discrimination and self-control. The horse represents the dynamic power of instinct, which energizes consciousness but which is sometimes liable to carry one away on a dangerously impetuous flight. The horse is the vitality of our earthy and biologically oriented existence; it supports its rider, which is our rational and spiritual power of waking consciousness.

After having lived a life of moral perfection and having received rigorous intellectual training, young Gregory has suddenly become the victim of uncontrollable impulses. His discovery that he was a foundling has released in him a desire to become a knight, a craving that he had never mentioned before. His knighthood fantasy has been lying in the unconscious, waiting to be released by just the right triggering influence, in this case, Gregory's sudden impulse to strike his brother.

Gregory wants to wield a lance, sword, and shield astride a fast horse, to do battle with an adversary while proving his bravery, manliness, and skill. He wants to fight for honor and glory. He also wants to find out who he is and where he came from.

Gregory has lost all interest and motivation in becoming a monk of the cloister. He is off and running! He has not the slightest hesitation or worry about how he will manage in this new role. He seems to fear nothing. This is typical of the hero.

Many young people are like this. The worst crime parents can commit is to try to pound sense into their children by relentlessly correcting their rather fantastic idealizations. It is better to be enthusiastic and supportive, which will probably stimulate a cautious reaction in the teenager. Young people need to follow their impulses long enough to test their self-confidence and powers of invention. Their projected dreams and fantasies are functioning to lead them away from home into the exciting and promising new world of their own future lives.

Parents should resist the temptation to supplant their child's farfetched motivations by their own commonsense experience, simply because they "know better." The very worst response parents can offer their child, the capital crime, is to wait until a child has failed and then say, "I told you so!" Failure is as real and as legitimate a part of life as success. It needs to be acknowledged and even respected. Learning to keep one's dignity and to respect it in others as one acknowledges failure is a great step toward a profounder appreciation of life.

What is interesting about Gregory's excitement is that he has received no actual training for knighthood, nor has he encountered many typical knights while sequestered in his isolated island convent. At first he lost control and struck his brother. Now he wants to become a professional fighter.

Psychologically he has been seized by an energy that drives him out of his familiar context into a much wider atmosphere, leaving behind everything that has informed his life up until then. He has learned that his life did not originate on the island, and he feels that he properly belongs somewhere else. But where? He desires to reconnect with that other life, which now seems more real and imperative to him. His stay with the fisherman's family and his cloister schooling seem to have been merely a temporary interruption—a displacement of his actual life—since he was consigned to the sea. It is now time to get back to business. This conviction has seized him in an instant.

Teenagers are typically like this, but so are we adults sometimes, when we are contending with a crisis involving a major transition in our lives. One morning a person wakes up and says to himself, "Where have I been all my life?" There is a lot of worry and then some new energy, and big changes are made. The person may change his or her job, spouse, philosophy of life, style of living, or even his or her personality. He thinks he is reconnecting to the *real* life that has always been his own but that got sidetracked, forgotten, or just yesterday appeared for the first time.

It is as if one lost one's way without knowing it, and then suddenly became aware of the problem. Such an awakening is very hard on those with whom one lives, because of the violent upheaval that ensues. And it is fraught with danger, as we shall see.

The old abbot is frightened by Gregory's impetuosity and urges the boy to remain on the island and sacrifice his big plans in order not to risk the loss of heaven after he dies. He fears that Gregory will forfeit his immortal soul and end up damned for eternity if he becomes entangled in worldly affairs. How strange this sounds to our modern ears!

Up through the Christian Middle Ages, most people didn't believe that a human life could be completed or fully realized on the face of this earth. That was reserved for the life hereafter, if one were lucky enough to escape the seductive snares of sinful pleasure, power, and worldly success in this "vale of tears," the secular realm in which we all must temporarily reside. Such a displacement of human potential onto an imaginary afterlife of purgatory and heaven has largely come to an end in our modern era. To many contemporary folk, such "pie in the sky" beliefs seem to be positively tragic and wasteful superstitions, even delusions, which were foisted upon poor and ignorant people as a means of gaining power and profit.

Jungian psychology has opposed this Marxist economic prejudice and other forms of psychological materialism. Gods, angels, devils, purgatories, heavens, hells, and all the rest are not
simply the contrived tools of social manipulation and repression. Neither are they merely psychological "defense mecha-
nisms" or childish fantasy, but are rather the outward
projections of innate spiritual facts in the archetypal unconscious that lie beyond the boundary of human ego consciousness. For Jung, such spiritual and metaphysical considerations
are just as real, just as much empirical facts, now as they were
in the Middle Ages, only with a slight shift of emphasis down-
ward and inward. No longer literal and concrete regions or
beings functioning in the space-time of outward scientific actuality, they seem now to be symbols of profoundly dynamic
inward psychological energies. They are facts of what Jung later
called the "objective psyche," the archetypal or nonpersonal
level of the deeper personality. But, as Jung never tired of
reminding his conservative religious critics, these inward realities are far from being *merely* psychological, for what is archetypally inner is not of "me" or "mine." It is of "Thou," or
sometimes even of the strangely impersonal and numinous "It."

Earlier we suggested that getting ensnared in the "world" has
the psychological meaning of following projections outside of
one's psyche, losing a direct awareness of self as an immediate
experience. The abbot was afraid that Gregory would lose his
immortal soul to this world. But such a contemplative wisdom is
more suited to a person in midlife; it has certain dangers for a boy
or girl just setting forth.

Modern young people must indeed follow such projections into
the world, for although many of these idealized longings will later
prove to be illusory, they are what give a young person the
impetus to leave the realm of childhood and the narrower security
of family. It is time to explore the wider landscape of experience
with its adventures, challenges, and promises. If the abbot had
had his way, Gregory would have remained sequestered in the

comfortable womb of Holy Mother Church, protected from the possibility of serious mortal sin and of what to him would seem to be any wider experience of life.

To Gregory, it would have been a veritable death of his spirit to have remained within the cloister. In similar fashion, James Joyce's Stephen Daedalus left the childhood atmosphere of his Roman Catholic youth, with its promise of a brilliant career in the priesthood, because he feared that he would die in that same womb:

> His soul had arisen from the grave of boyhood spurning her graveclothes. Yes! Yes! Yes! He would create proudly out of the freedom and power of his soul, as the great artificer whose name he bore, a living thing, new and soaring and beautiful, impalpable, imperishable.[1]

And if young Stephen needed any more to inspire him, it was not long before he encountered it on the beach in the person of a lovely girl. Her skirts were hiked up around her waist as she waded in the shallow water of a tidal rivulet. Stephen, completely arrested by the sensuous beauty and demeanor of this classical anima figure, stood gazing at her for several minutes,

> . . . and when she felt the presence and the worship of his eyes, her eyes turned to him in quiet sufferance of his gaze, without shame or wantonness.[2]

And Stephen, in an ecstasy, turned and strode away down the beach.

> Her image had passed into his soul for ever and no word had broken the holy silence of his ecstasy. Her eyes had called him and his soul had leaped at the call. A wild angel had appeared to him, the angel of mortal youth and beauty, an envoy from the fair courts of life, to throw open before him in an instant of ecstasy the gates of all the ways of error and glory. On and on and on and on![3]

To follow such impulses as we have described in the case of Gregory or Stephen would have unnerved any Christian monk in those days. Christians were didactically exhorted to "put on the new man," the "old man" being interpreted as the more natural personality, which lives primarily from the impulses of the fleshly body with its sanguine urges.

So unlike his father-uncle, who followed the advice of the old duke's counselor, Gregory spurns the monkish warning of the abbot and impetuously chooses the adventurous life of an errant knight. Have not many of us followed in his footsteps today?

In medieval times the expression *knight-errant* indicated a gentleman warrior who wandered with no specific destination, somewhat randomly in search of opportunities for heroic and valorous deeds. The relative aimlessness of such a knight's journeying is the reason for the epithet *errant*, which means to stay outside the proper path or bounds. It is related to the word *error*, meaning an ignorant or imprudent deviation from the code.

Gregory's task will be to break new ground, where apparently no one has ventured before. He is, we must recall, no ordinary youth, but is living in the service of the solar-hero archetype, so that he is destined to walk right out of the old dying forms and participate directly in the realization of the new. He is a revolutionary figure, furthering and completing for a time our destiny as human beings. From the conventional point of view, he will seem to be in "error."

However important it may seem for Gregory to go off and explore the world, we should not be naively optimistic about his "errant" desires. Such things are not simply black and white. The projections that lead a young person out into the world also cause untold suffering, pain, and disillusionment. This is because, at some level, there is an unreality about them. Projections are also illusions, and as one follows them, it is only a matter of time before one runs head-on up against a hard, even shocking reality.

It is for this reason that the religious traditions of the world have often tried to prevent the error from occurring by keeping children throughout their lives within the protective custody of a system of symbolic images and ceremonies. Taking a child into the monastery at a young age and keeping him there for life has not been unknown. The Fourteenth Dalai Lama, for instance, one of the foremost spiritual leaders of the world today, is a product of such a spiritual incarceration. Chosen from the cradle to be the supreme leader of Tibetan Buddhism, he was never given the opportunity to explore the world on his own, experiment with relationships, or freely choose a career. His vocation and all the circumstances of his future existence were ordained by others from the moment of his birth according to strict metaphysical and auguristic principles. He grew to adulthood with no "personal" life in the modern and Western sense of this term. His whole life has been confined almost exclusively to an archetypal or transpersonal existence. This is generally the case for all people of traditional societies.

The purpose of this kind of structuring is to put a person into a safe and orderly contact with the archetypal realm of experience so that his ego consciousness may be related directly to the symbols of transpersonal reality. Otherwise, in wandering the world or in experimenting with life (as he follows his projected fantasies), he may become subtly victimized by illusion and the seductiveness of his impulses, and fall into error unconsciously. He will then "act out" rather than become truly aware of his own true inner Self or of the objective empirical world surrounding him.

It was in this spirit that Jung envisioned the great religious traditions of the world as psychotherapeutic systems, guarding the mental and spiritual health of all those for whom such symbolic images and rituals still resonated in the heart and soul of the inner person.

The incestuous hero-path is laid out clearly and succinctly in each of the great world religions. The medieval celibate monk Gregory could have participated in it safely and nonliterally through medieval Catholic spirituality and the rich symbolism of the mass, where every Sunday, if not daily, to the sublime strains of plainsong chant and amid clouds of incense, the mysterious and paradoxical conception, birth, life, suffering, death, descent into hell, resurrection from the dead, and ascension into heaven of the "Sun of Righteousness"[4] was elaborately celebrated under symbolic form at the altar.

James Joyce turned his back on the religion of his youth and made a daring escape from the secure shelter of his Roman Catholic myth. He wandered the world as an expatriate, moving from place to place more than forty times during his adult life, living seven times in four different European cities. Joyce lived the life of a kind of literary knight-errant. He died in his fifties, a nearly blind alcoholic. One of his two children became an incurable schizophrenic and the other an alcoholic whose career never really blossomed. Joyce is considered the preeminent literary artist of our century, but he "wandered" from his Dublin home and from the religious structures of his youth. What a price he and his family paid for his genius. From a strictly personal point of view, one may wonder if it was worthwhile for him to choose the way of "error." Was he a failed hero? Was he trapped in the belly of the night-sea monster? How much do many of *us* have in common with him?

After Gregory's tearful parting with his godfather, the abbot, we hear no more of this kindly old priest. Nor is there any hint later on, after Gregory completes his adventures, that the old abbot ever learns the outcome. This clerical gentleman is a symbol of the old era, of the age that is drawing to a close. He will have no share in the exciting but dangerous new psychological world of true knighthood, which is already beginning to develop, namely the possibility of an individual interiority of consciousness that honors the feminine.

As hero, Gregory must enter the dark and dangerous nether realm to find the great boon, to learn the ineffable wisdom, to unlock the secret of life, and then bring it safely back to waking consciousness, so that the world might learn from his experience and teaching, and thereby be rejuvenated and carried forward to a period of new and creative living. Whether we realize it or not, Gregory functions within us today.[5]

"Gregory" is the only proper name mentioned in Hartmann's entire poem of four thousand and six lines. His name derives from a Greek etymological root that means "vigilant" or "awake." It is an apt name for a type of solar hero who will bring new consciousness and a brighter vision of life. It is also a name applicable to us, insofar as we may awaken to the death and resurrection of our capacity for living.

Gregory's parents were born as their own mother died. Later, Gregory himself came into the world, but he was immediately consigned to a death-and-rebirth ordeal in his perilous night-sea journey, which landed him on the abbot's island. Shortly after his rescue from the ocean waves, he was immersed in the waters of baptism, another symbolic night-sea journey of death and regeneration. Then, when he had grown through childhood and successfully established himself as a scholar of promise and good reputation, he had to endure the death experience of learning that he was a foundling boy with dark and dubious origins.

Taking permanent leave of everything familiar, Gregory begins yet another new life, the fifth to emerge in our tale. There will yet be two more before Gregory's story is finished, making seven in all.[6]

As we contemplate the erstwhile monk Gregory leaving the monastery and going off with his horse to begin life as a traveling knight, we should remind ourselves that what we have been taught concerning the "Christianization" of Europe was in many instances a rather superficial matter.

The early missionaries might convert a bellicose chieftain or marauding warrior-king under mostly political circumstances, often by threat of the sword, and then all the underlings and peasants were required to follow suit summarily, by receiving baptism. It is obvious that this sort of piety touched only the most superficial layers of the European psyche. Far too often it proved to be a form of coercion. Below the surface, and kept in suppression by the loftier religious ethic of peace, love, and self-sacrifice, were the old brutal impulses to war, pillage, rape, and conquer by wild and blatant force. The average Christian of the twelfth century was no doubt a vulgar savage with a mask or persona of godliness in the Christian style. It held primitive and beastly strivings in check only partially and temporarily through rigorous self-control and a severe threat of punishment. At any moment the old savage impulses could and did break out. And since these impulses had been rather severely repressed by the new Christian ethic, when they occasionally *did* explode, it was with a remarkable crudity and intensity.

A notorious example, reported by Nicetas Choniates in Constantinople during the course of the fourth Crusade in 1204, depicted a Christian army sacking the great Orthodox Cathedral of the Hagia Sophia (Christ as "Holy Wisdom"). They desecrated the high altar, pillaged the church of precious works of art, threw the Blessed Sacrament into a sewer, cast relics into the gutter, and installed a common harlot on the episcopal throne of the Patriarch, where she sang blasphemous songs degrading the Christian Savior and then performed lewd dances in the sacred places of the church, while the nuns and townswomen were raped.[7]

These were Christian soldiers, on a Christian Crusade headed by the cross, doing violence in a Christian shrine. They spent so much time pillaging and looting the citizens of Constantinople that they never arrived at their destination, the Holy Land.

One suspects that few people in the Middle Ages had gone the full route of real transformation of instinct to any very deep level. Only the upper level had become nominally "Christian." Are we any different?

Our tale is concerned with a much deeper and more wholistic transformation of instinct than nominal religiosity. It concerns the joining of heaven and earth, of the spiritual aspirations *and* earthly instincts to create a new integral humanity that is consciously aware and sensitive to life, not a mere brute held under control by guilt or threats of punishment.

In arguing with the abbot, Gregory says that he has always longed more for the spear than for the stylus, and that the sword is more dear to him than any pen could be. Gregory senses that the scholarly world of the pen must give way to the spear and the sword, the more primitive masculine implements. These must be fully developed before a higher and more civilized consciousness is possible. The sword impulses must come first, and only then may they be transformed, or evolved into the pen, which may serve as the weapon of the mind. The more primitive instinct cannot be skipped over, or suppressed, in the hopes of substituting the peaceful life of the scholar in its stead.

A young man, and the animus in woman, must grow through successive stages from the more primitive to a more cultivated and refined human consciousness. First comes the brute power of animal vitality. Then an earthy masculinity of the hunter and warrior, followed by a dashing lover or courtier phase. Later comes the higher and more sublimated activity of the scholar, the poet, the philosopher, or the mystic. Gregory would be missing several stages if he were to adopt the attitude and lifestyle of a monk before meeting the challenges of a rougher and more vigorous sort, in order to make conscious his primitive masculinity.

If a boy is pushed too quickly toward gentleness, thoughtfulness, good manners, refinement, or aesthetic and moral sensitivity, and not encouraged to indulge his more red-blooded "rascal" side, he will lack a certain earthy manliness. He will turn out to be the mealy-mouthed darling, an effeminate, domesticated, or overly educated "nerd." He may have grace and intelligence but little force or direct substance in his character. Instinctive behavior must be encouraged at appropriate levels, then evolved to higher applications, so that the original impulses are not damaged or banished altogether to the unconscious. At this level they will simply flare up at certain inopportune moments or, on occasion, cause illness. My son had to go through his "I'm a tough guy" act when he was six years old, with that flashing gleam in his narrowed eyes that I remember so well.

The spear and the sword are not just instruments of lethal harm. Symbolically they represent the development of certain psychological powers connected with the function of masculine consciousness.

The spear, or lance, suggests aim, or the life urge that leads forward toward a clearly marked objective. The use of the spear is related to the masculine ability to keep one's eye on the target as one moves forward in life.

The sword signifies a similar type of commitment, which carries the meaning of strength, power, the capability of "cutting through," of differentiating one thing from another. With the sword one cuts through to the core of a problem or dilemma, discarding whatever is irrelevant to the overall purpose.

In short, the spear represents purposefulness and bold intuition, the sword, clear-minded understanding. Passivity, confusion, hesitation, and fuzzy-headedness are overcome at this stage of development, which leads to perceptive intuition and rational comprehension.[8] In the psyche of a woman these capabilities are available to her through the animus, but only if she is already securely rooted in her own femininity. If she is not, her masculine competence will appear in negative, distorted, or misplaced form.

One more word on the sword. In antiquity the sword was connected with the power of the sun. In the old mythic images the rays of the sun were depicted as sharp swords that brought the clarity of vision needed for consciousness.

In the apocalyptic vision of Saint John at the end of the New Testament, a powerful figure with flaming white hair, shining like the sun, and intensely burning eyes is depicted emitting a sharp sword from his mouth. This was interpreted as the "Word," or the masculine Spirit of God, which would render a judgment on the entire world.[9]

This solar attribute of his weapon of choice connects Gregory again to the hero journey of renewed and renewing consciousness, like the sun, which travels through the underworld waters of the abyss, ultimately to burst its bonds and rise triumphantly as the eastern morning. The Roman emperors took this symbolism as an attribute and epithet, employing the title Sol Invictus, "The Invincible Sun." Gregory is headed in this same direction through his night-sea journey to a new day.

After parting from the abbot, Gregory prays to God for direction and aid, and then tells his helmsman to follow a course that the winds will design, and to steer blindly. A strong gale blows up, and after three days Gregory and his crew are driven near the shore of a new land. His larger destiny is being accomplished through the agency of a mysterious and invisible force of nature, the wind.

With astounding naiveté, we Westerners, equating religion with conventional morality and goodness, believe that to be a "holy person" means to practice a conforming religiosity.

But at the deeper psychological levels, precisely the *opposite* is true. When Gregory follows the wind, rather than a navigational chart or even his own personal perception of which way to steer, he is following the inspiration of a spiritual power that is *beyond* human conventions, categories of thought, and morality. it is fair to say that "God," as profoundly and actually experienced, rather than as a topic of creedal belief, is beyond morality, beyond good and evil, beyond existence and nonexistence, all of which are all purely human and therefore limited concepts of the mind.

Gregory has spurned the good advice and warnings of his fatherly superior and has gone off willy-nilly on a strange and uncanny adventure, never to return to the abbot, or to what that cleric represents. He will never be "normal," "perfect," or well-adjusted again, but quite the opposite.

A transcendent power of the archetypal unconscious has carried him away:

> Do not be surprised when I say: You must be born from above. The wind blows wherever it pleases; you hear its sound but you cannot tell where it comes or where it is going. That is how it is with all who are born of the Spirit. [10]

NINE

THE SUN OF HER DELIGHT

As they sail past the coastline, Gregory and his crew sight a besieged city and a scorched and devastated land. Gregory orders his crew to change sail and steer toward shore.

Unwittingly, Gregory is arriving at his mother's realm, which had been invaded some years earlier by the jealous duke who had pleaded unsuccessfully for the lady's hand.

When Gregory learns of her sorry predicament, he wants to defend the beautiful duchess by engaging her foe.

Gregory asks the palace steward how he can gain an audience with the lady. Because of her joyless grief, the duchess has made it her practice to appear to no friend or guest except in the cathedral, where she goes every day to stand in prayer.

In the church the steward presents Gregory to the duchess, recommending the boy to her as an honorable knight. The lady looks upon this handsome youth—her own child—as a stranger.

She is much taken with him, and her heart beats with emotion. She gazes at him longer than she has ever looked at any man before, and notices the rich pattern of fine silk he wears. It is familiar to her, so much like the brocade she had placed in the chest with her little son so many years ago.

Gregory and the duchess are very pleased with each other. When the audience is ended and they part, Gregory's heart goes with her. From this moment on, Gregory chooses more than ever to pursue a life of fame and glory. He is extremely happy, realizing that all of life's joys are nearly his.

Gregory practices jousting and becomes the most able knight in the realm, earning much fame and glory.

Meanwhile, the lady's fierce suitor has earned himself a formidable reputation, having defeated one knight after another before the gate to her citadel, until none are left to defend the duchess's honor. This single knight has laid a whole army low!

Gregory decides to risk everything in one throw and cast his very life into the balance in a flagrant attempt to defeat the duchess's unwelcome suitor. "I would rather meet death bravely and live a short life with honor than live a longer life in mediocrity," he exclaims.

A few days later, Gregory enters the field against the jealous duke. As they spar, Gregory subtly entices his adversary back toward the gate of the lady's citadel. Now they fight in deadly earnest. The crashing and clanging of steel are heard. Their lances shatter, and they fight now with swords until the duke is disarmed. Gregory grabs the bridle of the duke's horse and pulls both man and beast back through the gate of the citadel, which the duchess's men hastily close against the duke's army. Holding the defeated suitor hostage, Gregory and the duchess extract a surrender with generous terms of reparation for all the damage done during the long siege.

Gregory is the hero of the day, showered with glory and honor.

After the celebrations have passed, the lady's barons encourage her to choose a husband to end the duchy's vulnerability to future suitors. "It would be better," they say, "if a strong man ruled over us, and besides, the duchy needs an heir."

The lady casts about for a good prospect and has no trouble settling upon Gregory! This pleases everyone, including the duchess and her knight, who are already deeply in love and devoted to one another. They are married amid jubilant celebration. Gregory is made sovereign lord of the land, rules exceedingly well, and is a popular and most noble head of state.

Gregory is now happier than he thought it possible for any human being to be in this world, and he wants for nothing. It seems to him that God has graced him with every favor imaginable. For Gregory, life is now pure bliss.

As Gregory left the island monastery, he ordered his crew to steer blindly and allow the wind to govern their course. The wind serves as a symbol for the invisible Spirit, since in Greek, the name for both "spirit" and "wind" is *pneuma*. The Spirit has "regressed" (from Latin *re*, "back," and *gradi*, "step"), that is, it has carried Gregory back to his place of origin. The Spirit of God has led him back to his own mother's country, where his thirst for glorious deeds and honor has driven him straight into her arms.

Without realizing what he is doing, Gregory unwittingly breaks the severest taboo, the moral law against incest.

We must remember that the lady made a solemn vow to marry no mortal man, but rather "he who has been loved since time began." She courted Jesus Christ through prayer, fastings, chastity, and good works, and became a joyless recluse nun in her own palace. She became a "bride of Christ."

In the Middle Ages, women who entered convents expressed their solemn vow to God by pledging to live in poverty, chastity, and obedience. They wore a wedding ring and veil, symbolizing their "spiritual" marriage to Christ. This transformation of their sexuality and love to another symbolic level of experience is what psychologists call sublimation.

Both Freud and Jung agreed that the sublimation of incest is what produces culture and consciousness in human nature. They differed greatly, however, in defining more precisely the meaning and significance of sublimation. We shall return to this interesting subject in chapter 12.

A nun commonly modeled her life on the faith and devotional ideal of the Virgin Mary. But at the same time she conceived of her spiritual vocation as a nuptial union with Christ. This amounts to a symbolic marriage of mother with son. Its ultimate purpose is the spiritual creation of a contemplative interior field of awareness, a greater consciousness in the womblike ground of being of the psyche. It is the specific Christian version of the night-sea journey.

In the beginning, when the duchess sent her infant son away in the chest, she expressed her wish that he become a religious man and devote himself to intercessory prayer in behalf of his sinful parents. She hoped that knowledge of his origin might keep him from arrogance. Such a religious life would normally have taken the form of a monastic existence in the Middle Ages, with full access to the *symbols* and *rituals* of regression and regeneration. In the mythic images of the Church, the Father and the Son are of "one substance,"[1] and the Virgin is both the Bride of God and the Mother of God.

Most Christians are shocked to learn that an incestuous current of symbolism lies at the very heart of their faith and devotion. How illuminating is the following epigram of Giovanni Battista Strozzi the Elder, concerning Christ and addressed to the Virgin:

> He is also, in spite of Himself,
> Our Lord and thy
> Spouse, son, and father,
> O His only spouse, daughter, and mother.[2]

But Gregory's mother gave him the gold and the silk brocade, which enabled him to become a worldly knight and wander in "error" back to her again. She equipped Gregory with the real means to accomplish a concrete regression. In the night-sea journey, this would be the stage when the radiant sun hero begins his westward descent toward the underworld ocean, to the place of his origin, where the grave and the womb are a single paradoxical reality. In our tale, however, the knightly form of regression is actual. Gregory as ego-man commits incest with his personal flesh-and-blood mother.

Gregory left the monastery, where he might have continued to rightfully sublimate his incestuous longings. He might have accomplished this through the religious symbolism of the *hieros gamos*, or sacred marriage of Christ with his bride the Church, or by an introverted meditation upon the heavenly union of "the Second Adam," Christ, with "the Second Eve," Mary, who reign together as the King and Queen of Paradise.³ By leaving this highly charged *symbolic* environment and wandering the world, he made himself vulnerable to concrete and actual incest. His mother, even before Gregory's victory, began to take a passionate interest in him, in conflict with her religious vow. Then, after his victorious struggle with the invading duke, she agreed to marry a mortal man after all! They both relinquished the inward, spiritual, or symbolic level of incest, and then fell into it outwardly.

For his part, Gregory stopped far short of his original intention after he left the abbot. He wanted to find out who he was and where he came from. But at the first sight of land, he stopped off, fell intensely in love, got involved in glorious deeds, then settled down into an apparently comfortable and happy marriage, just as countless young people do today. Gregory never discovered who he was or where he came from. He remained in the first place he stopped, and thought he had attained the happiest life possible in this world.

For a man to disengage his energy and awareness from the mother complex entails far more than an outward separation from or avoidance of the woman who is his parent. The archetypal anima level of a man's psyche is given specific content through the combined inner and outer experience of the actual mother.

Many outward experiences of the mother are incorporated into the child's own personality. A man may carry his mother within him long after she has died outwardly. She lives on in him as a vague yearning for emotional satisfaction and fulfillment that seems to be around the very next bend in the road, or in that enchanting lady he met just last night.

If this inherent femininity, which is the potential realization of psychic interiority and well-being, remains unconscious, so that it does not contribute to a man's own experience of living, then it will be projected or "transferred" to some other person or situation in adult life. For instance, a man will find a surrogate mother in his wife. This may encourage an unpleasant dependency on his part and induce a reluctant solicitude in his mate. But it will be only a matter of time before the situation gives rise to irritating complications for both partners. His spouse will seem to have "changed," and he will begin fantasizing about another woman.

A certain kind of man seems destined never to achieve a satisfactory relation to a woman. Every woman who enters his orbit is expected to carry the whole load of feminine experience for him. He tries to live the whole erotic-feeling side of existence through her. An actual woman will be invested with unrealistically sublime qualities—she will have to be either the protective mother, the nubile maiden, the virginal saint, or the earthy whore for him. He will be unable to acknowledge her as the complete and ordinary human being she really is, with her particular interests, assets, and limitations. If a man has not become consciously allied to his inner feminine side, he will prove incapable of sharing equitable partnership with a flesh-and-blood woman. If he does not withdraw completely from erotic relations and fall into despondent melancholy, he will be continually "on the make," searching for the next ideal woman, who is sure to be "Ms. Right" this time.

It is the unconscious mother *within* that is the source of a man's tendency to become dependently contained by or to make unrealistic claims upon his partner. The solution of the mother-complex involvement inevitably entails some program of falling back upon his self-reliance and resourcefulness. Most people must learn to develop a certain amount of autonomy, not by adopting a persona of rugged individualism, but through developing a confidence in their ability to be at least moderately self-contained. They must learn to provide for their own emotional needs to some extent, to experience a fresh vitality within themselves, and to handle life's challenges as they present themselves day by day.

In our story, all this is condensed into the episode of Gregory's blind infatuation with his mother, his heroic defense of her, and his belief that he has finally laid claim to an incomparable happiness.

Gregory had been guided to the place where he might learn the answers to his pressing questions about his identity and origin—that is, learn with full consciousness the roots of his strange and uncommon life. He was precisely in the right place, but he never mentioned his mission to anyone nor asked any questions. Why was he suddenly so uncurious? And his mother, who recognized the pattern of silk brocade in his clothing, asked no questions about his origins. Apparently, Gregory kept his precious tablet and its contents a secret from everyone and never divulged that he was originally a princely outcast, the dark son of incest. Both mother and son remained completely unconscious.

There is an important and meaningful connection between not asking any obvious questions and the keeping of shameful secrets. When projections rule one's encounter with another person, there appears to be no need to ask questions, for the meaning and significance of that other is obvious. One makes a series of *assumptions* about people or things, believing them all to be the simple, unadulterated truth. In our lives, we are particularly prone to this kind of unconscious stupidity when we are unrealistically happy, enjoying a mighty period of success, or in a glorious "good mood." These are mother-complex symptoms.

When we are under the spell of these projections, illusory veils govern not only our perception of outer "reality," but also our experience of ourselves. Gregory appeared once again in his mother's land as a handsome, aristocratic, and wealthy knight. In worldly terms he was really *somebody*. But was he? What had happened to the "nobody," to the foundling who had been dragged out of the sea by the peasant fishermen? He was keeping this dimension of himself well hidden from the world, this private and embarrassing fact of his life. A "nobody" would have no chance of honor, fame, or great deeds, particularly a "nobody" engendered through incest. In the collective world of respectability, he was a reprobate, unclean, horrible, a virtual pariah. But all this was kept a secret, split off from Gregory's outward reputation as a shining hero who enjoyed the surface experience of romantic bliss.

When Gregory's mother packed the precious fabric and the gold with the tablet in the chest, she was contaminating his life with motives of her own. When, as a young knight, he wears clothing made from this fabric, he is functioning in the persona, or ideal role, that his mother wishes for him. Rather than living his own life, he lives the one she needs him to live. His beautiful knightly outfit is a symbol of Gregory's mother complex. He will unwittingly attempt to be his mother's hero and therefore share in her inflation. He will become a "big man" in the world. He will "feel good" about himself. He will succeed. He will be compelled by his mother complex to attain this success.

The fortune of gold with which Gregory was endowed is itself an archetypal symbol. Gold is the metal and lion-color of royalty, and is synonymous with the brilliant radiance of the sun. In alchemy, gold represented both luminous consciousness and eternal life, the longed-for goal of the art.

Therefore, when Gregory puts on the aristocratic garments of silk and uses the gold to furnish himself with the means to travel in knightly style, he is functioning not as an ordinary human being, but in the character of an archetype; that is, he has taken on divine status. He is now the solar hero of the night-sea journey.

When Gregory's twin parents were orphaned and committed incest, they crossed the border into the archetypal realm, entered the Divine Bridal Chamber, and lost their simple human identities. It was as if their ordinary humanity had been absorbed into the royal-archetypal realm. This is psychological inflation, which, as we have seen, can make one feel either "high" or "low."

In a sense, the "fame" and "glory" that Gregory attained, and the blissful happiness that he enjoyed, are our own. When we are happy, in a "good mood," and "on top of the world," shouldn't we pause for thought? Isn't there more to this than meets the eye? We all have grown up in a culture that prizes "feeling good." Like Gregory, we keep our sadness and our problems about self-worth to ourselves and try to "make it" in the world. Few of us can tolerate the notion that somewhere underneath, we are peasant "nobodies," people who have no right to an inflated and grandiose life. This is because most of us are stuck in our mother complex.

Our story says that the duchess received no one in audience except when she stood in the cathedral, where she went each day to hear mass. Most cathedrals built in the twelfth century were dedicated to the Blessed Virgin Mary. As Henry Adams has reminded us, these prodigiously beautiful structures were conceived to be great palaces, serving as the earthly domiciles of the celestial Virgin Mother of God, the Queen of Heaven.[4] It has been estimated that in the twelfth century, the French alone spent the equivalent in today's currency of ten billion dollars on such colossal monuments.[5] This amounts to a staggering per-capita investment when we recall the relatively small population of Europe in those days. It is quite a revelation to note that the magnificent Cathedral of Notre Dame in Paris was financed and built by a population of merely seventy thousand souls, the equivalent in today's America of Bethlehem, Pennsylvania, or Terre Haute, Indiana. Our medieval ancestors felt inspired to build the most sublimely beautiful and the grandest residence possible, using the most up-to-date technology and crafts, in honor of their Heavenly Lady.

This was, in part, how our medieval ancestors dealt effectively with the mother complex. They separated the celestial or archetypal Mother, whom they venerated, from the earthly and personal one, whom they loved. It was much safer that way—and far healthier. Today, an ordinary woman is often asked to carry all this personally. It is simply too much for her to bear.

By choosing the cathedral as her reception chamber for official guests, one suspects that this duchess-nun is in fact identifying herself with the Queen of Heaven and is setting herself forth in this role as she encounters her people. That Gregory and his mother meet for the first time in the cathedral suggests that the archetype of the Madonna and Child will somehow inform their relationship. In a sense, she is also identifying herself with the Church, the medieval Holy Mother, the Bride of Christ. These are purely archetypal connections, not human ones.

When Gregory and his mother encountered each other in the cathedral, she viewed him as if he were a stranger. Her heart was blind as it beat, and she was unaware that the magnificent young man who stood before her was in fact her own son.

Gregory succeeded in marrying his mother, and the duchess her own son, without either of them realizing it. Then they were both on top of the world! Nothing could be better. Much of our lives today is full of this inflated spirit. We're all blown up into something far bigger than we have any right to be. There are many "Jesus Christs" and "Virgin Marys" walking the streets today!

When psychologists say that the mother complex governs the relationship between a man and a woman, they do not mean that there is necessarily any literal or physical sexual relationship between a mother and son. From the inner and archetypal point of view, "mother" is simply the instinctive unconscious psyche, "Mother Nature" in oneself, the animal state of purely instinctive-impulsive behavior and irresponsible dreaming fantasy. As a child grows to adulthood, he or she learns to oppose this naive unconsciousness of nature with an increasingly developed conscious awareness that can exercise discrimination, self-control, tenacity, goal achievement, insight, and responsibility. In a certain sense, the purpose of the incest taboo is to prevent one from letting go of these valuable cultural achievements in order to lapse back once again into the regressive and irresponsible state of nature. A flaming sword bars our way back to the paradise of Eden.

This so-called mother complex is an inner psychological structure that gives us our inherent sense of trust and an expectation of fulfillment. This is based on our fundamentally instinctive orientation in the natural world. To the extent that a person is regressively and personally entangled in this unconscious complex of feelings and ideas, he will expect the world to serve up life to him on a silver platter free of charge. He will remain a dependent child in all his dealings with life. The world itself is his mother, even her womb and her breast, which are taken for granted. He expects her (that is, everyone) to minister to him alone as the center of interest, fatefully giving him her bounty. Realistically, this takes the form of a relationship in which one person is "king" or "queen," and other people are "slaves." If things don't happen according to schedule, then rage, spectacular disappointment, a gnawing irritability, or an impulse toward insidious manipulation is the reaction, but never a sensible and self-responsible strategy that could promise an effective solution. Someone *else* is always responsible.

Whenever we harangue about what is "owed" to us, what we "deserve," or our inalienable "rights," we are in the middle of our mother complex. When we say, "*They* ought to change this, fix that, reform the other thing," or when we blame this person or that thing in our lives, it is a sign that our mother complex is peeking around the edges of our consciousness.

Behind all our adult cravings for progress, success, achievement, and happiness stands this glorious mystery of the all-embracing and -sustaining Mother-Madonna. It is She who raises Her lamp "beside the golden door"[6] of our hopes and dreams.

Sometimes the mother complex may be negative. Then a serious problem of trust, either of the environment or of one's own self, results in a loss of one's confidence and optimism toward life.

Daughters have a somewhat different relation to the mother-complex problem than sons. When the problem is positive, then a woman may overdevelop her own mother-qualities and identify herself totally as the nourisher and container of her brood, including her husband and pets. She will develop no individual life of her own, and will instinctively live through her family and identify completely with its general interests and concerns.

Or, if this complex is negative, the daughter may very well develop her own personality as an individual, particularly in relation to intellect, career, other people outside the family, or spiritually, but suffer a severe lack of maternal instincts. She will purposefully avoid interests or investments that would require her to sustain domestic and maternal obligations. [7]

In the first case, the woman will be sunk in maternal instinct, but with little development of her own personality. In the second, the earthy maternal side will be suppressed in favor of independence, action in the world, a series of fleeting romances, or intellectual achievement.

Gregory is a special example of such a mother-bound state which Jungians call the *puer aeternus*, the eternal youth. This is a complex found in the personalities of both men and women. (In women it is often known as the *puella aeterna*.) Such a person is convinced that his or her own life and its destiny are indeed special, that it is equipped with an unusual fatefulness that draws that person forward in an exciting adventure that has sublime heroic qualities. One's success and happiness are "meant to be."

An immature puer is very prone to reject the value of "here and now" reality. The ordinary and stable round of domestic and familiar routines, and of long-lasting and habitual existence in common with others, is devalued. Stability and security soon become a veritable prison to such a person. He or she must be on the way toward what is grandly promised, as if mysteriously preordained from on high. The next place or achievement is just too exciting, too full of mysterious possibilities and further heights, while the present circumstances are far too boringly familiar, mundane, or limiting. However, the puer complex can have a very positive function in the psyche. It is full of volatile heroic energy, enthusiasm, and optimism. It will not hesitate to break with the dead weight of past conventions and search for something new.

A woman may experience all this unconsciously and project it onto her son, rather than following any of these exciting and promising impulses in her own life.

These puers are the people who demand the freedom to "pick up their marbles and go" whenever the spirit moves them. The future is theirs. They have big plans! They get itchy if they become settled for too long. Domestic life is not for them, except when it suits their dependent needs for comfort, pleasure, or convenience. If they enter psychotherapy, they often terminate prematurely.

What this often amounts to is the internalization of the mother's own ambitions, which have been unrealized. Because these ambitions have remained essentially unconscious in the personality of the mother herself, they have been projected upon the son, inducing in him the secret hope and ambition that she has *for him*. Such a boy grows up to attempt the achievement of his mother's aspirations, naively believing them to be his own.

A man in his late forties had the following dream at a time when he was feeling a gnawing depression over his lack of success:

I find myself high on an enormous bridge tower that spans a river. I am dizzy with fright at being so high. I look down hundreds of feet below me and notice that the entire bridge tower is suspended in midair. It has no foundation in the river bed. To escape I would have to climb down as low on the tower as possible, then drop a hundred feet or so into the water. I am paralyzed with fear. I look up toward the very top of this tower, and I see my mother sitting on the very peak of it.

This is an excellent example of an inflation dream. The whole bridge is up in the air, which means in the archetypal realm of the transpersonal masculine spirit. It is "supernatural," above the level of ordinary earthly experience, and has virtually no connection to it. It has no foundation in real and ordinary life. Such a man would be quite spaced out, farfetched and abstract in his attitude. His feet would not appear to be on the ground, psychologically. The dreamer's mother was a highly intelligent and creative woman who did not develop her own professional and intellectual skills but remained at home, performed her mother role dutifully though reluctantly, and often fantasized about what "might have been."

The dream demonstrates that the man's inflation is fueled by his mother complex, meaning that he is striving to reach a sublime success according to his mother's fantasy, a notion that probably comes from her undeveloped and unconscious animus, always an airy spirit. The dream is frightening the man's ego attitude in order to force him out of his inflatedness. He would do well to simply give up this tower and the upward striving it signifies, and jump! This would save him. It would solve his depressiveness and lack of self-esteem. It might even put a foundation under the bridge! In a dream it is very safe to jump. Just the first step toward reality is enough to solve the entire problem and make everything safe.

A puer complex may be relatively positive for young people, because it propels them out of the nest into the world of experiences beyond the family and beyond the commonplace vapidities of life. It helps them to "think big" and develop a passion for achievement. However, it can also assume the form of rash presumption, inordinate ambition, and inflated pride, as a youth takes aim at the very stars.

The gold and the precious fabric that Gregory's mother sent along in the chest were not earned or consciously chosen by him. They were his mother's endowment to him as she mused upon his destiny while he was still a tiny infant. His courage and heroism served not his own interests, but his mother's. The fact that he ended up marrying her is proof of the ultimate aim of these strivings.

Gregory has a relatively simple-minded and uncompromising need for excitement and adventure and a need to test and prove himself. "I would rather meet death bravely and live a short life with honor," says Gregory, "than live a longer life in mediocrity." Gregory is his mother's son, not his own man.

The puer is well symbolized by the newly risen sun that ceaselessly climbs to the heights of midday. Afternoon and evening have no place in such a scheme of things. Gregory is both the "son" and the "sun" of his mother's delight, the fiery energy of a new day, a radiant God, ascending the sky toward the apogee of his brilliant achievement.

Gregory fully believes that he has ventured forth into the new and wide world, and through resolute and heroic action has accomplished a supremely good deed by entering a foreign territory, defeating a belligerent duke, and saving a beautiful duchess's realm from total destruction. And he has won as his prize the first and only love of his life, and gained an entire realm in the bargain. He is on top of the world. He possesses everything a man could hope for.

We know differently, of course. In reality he has simply regressed to the primal condition of the child with his mother. The archetypal Virgin Mother of God and personal mother have become one and the same. Our story is giving us the psychological fact of a modern person's developing spiritual life. At this point our hero is like the widely produced medieval image, a typical focus of the Gothic twelfth century, of the infant Jesus, holding the orb and scepter of the world in his tiny hands, while enthroned in the lap of his beautifully serene queen-Madonna mother.[8]

What about the duchess's insistent suitor? The warring duke didn't just charge in immediately. He pleaded and pleaded for the lady's hand, and it was only after repeated refusals and cold rebuffs that his attitude became belligerent.

Symbolically this jealous duke may represent a current of psychic energy that moves *out* into the world, away from the hinterlands of the psyche. His fascination with the lovely duchess drew him beyond the borders of his own geographical realm toward a goal of marriage to a woman of *other* blood. His utterly nonincestuous marriage to the lady would bring "new blood" into the life of his kingdom, and "new blood" into hers as well.

This geographical impulse toward outward expansion, exploration, and achievement is a symbol of psychological extraversion, the movement of interest and energy beyond the borders of self-absorption to fresh new experiences and encounters in the exterior theater of events. This stance is precisely the psychological opposite of introversion (symbolic incest), integration, union with the Self, and consolidation and reinforcement of the inherent psyche.

But Gregory subdues the duke, and in the strangest fashion he grabs hold of him and refuses to let go. Then he urges his horse *backward* toward his mistress's gate, dragging the duke *inside* the walls of her citadel, and taking him prisoner there. It is a victory by regress. This noble hostage is subsequently employed as leverage for a favorable settlement.

In having pulled the duke back inside the walls as a prisoner, Gregory has functioned to introvert all the libido, or psychic energy, which is available, turning it away from the outer realm of worldly experience toward the interior regions of the psyche. His interest and attention remain in the service of the mother, who symbolizes his origin. All the exogamous energy is inhibited and redirected toward the mother depths, where it is captured. His interest serves the endogenous principle, which is attention regressively turned inward.

But if all the extraverted male energy is now contained within the lady's duchy, in a relation of son to mother, in what sort of condition or health are masculinity and consciousness? They are essentially unconscious and mother-bound.

As long as it remains this way, there can be no conscious standpoint that is distinct from the feminine matrix of the psyche. Gregory, like Oedipus, is oblivious to the real import of his actions. In order to function as a successful hero, he would have to enter upon a regressive inward journey with wide-awake appreciation of his motives and actions. Like the sun in the underworld, Gregory would have to shed light on the dark incestuous depths of the psyche. But this phenomenon of illumination has not yet occurred. With the unwelcome suitor as his captive, Gregory plunges blindly into the somber abyss of sin and death. He is completely in the dark.

Gregory is absolutely unconscious of his real circumstances. He himself believes he has gone out into the big wide world and earned something independent and achieved something of great masculine value for himself. But he is painfully and exactly wrong! He has gone *in*, not *out*.

To go in while realizing the full implication of one's attitude is contemplative wisdom, or insight. To go in unawares is the childish and neurotic foolishness of the mother complex. The apocryphal Gospel of Thomas, with a slightly different emphasis, has Jesus say, "If you bring forth what is inside you, what you bring forth will save you. If you do not bring forth what is inside you, what you do not bring forth will destroy you."[9]

The key to incest in our story has to do precisely with this clash of inside-outside realities. Jung employed the terms *exogamous* and *endogenous*, which Freud had also used, in a new way. He was intrigued with a paper by the British anthropologist and analyst John Layard, entitled "The Incest Taboo and the Virgin Archetype" (1945),[10] which alluded to various clan-oriented marriage classes among tribal peoples. In the settings to which Layard alluded, people were required to marry cousins who belonged to families on the mother's side. The regulations required a certain degree of consanguinity, but not closer than a prescribed orbit. This served to build up a cohesion of blood-related clans, but also to avoid too direct or close an incestuous matrimony. Thus the consanguineous family was both united to itself and attuned to the society at large.

Jung understood such marriage taboos as more than just sociological or ethical categories of behavior. He saw them also as expressions of a fundamental archetypal principle in the psyche, which governs the introverted and extraverted tendencies in the personality and keeps them in a healthy balance.

Jung's sense of the dynamism of psychic energy was that the human being lives in a double environment. One is the external world of society and the surrounding cosmos. The other is the interior world of the archetypes, the microcosmic inner facts of our psychological Ground of Being.[11] For Jung, a workable adaptation must be made to both regions, the outer and the inner. Both are real, both are legitimate objects of our fear, desire, respect, and inquiry. The interior images and events of imagination and dream are also a reality with which we must reckon. True health, according to Jung, results from an attitude that is able to accommodate itself to both regions at once.

Jung made the further observation that the extraverted, or exogamous, task is generally the typical emphasis during the first half of life, while the introverted, or endogenous, task is the challenge for persons on the second half of their life's journey: "what the youth found and must find outside, the man of middle life must find within himself."[12]

It is precisely this "within" that is the object of any introverted or incestuous current of interest. Jung never tired of referring to the ubiquitous appearance of mother symbols. Consciousness is born out of the unconscious womb of life and longs to return to it once again. In fact it does, every night when we fall asleep, and when the introverted cycle takes over completely and we dream about the interior landscape of our own souls.

Joseph Campbell liked to use the expression "from the tomb of the womb to the womb of the tomb." It is a death and a neurotic regression to return to the interior depths while still a child, for that is precisely the psychological mother-incest, which deludes and entraps the growing consciousness of the youth. But in later years, when the ego is strong yet not inflated, a journey down into the depths is possible. This may be accomplished through a more detached and meditative attitude, the serious study of one's dreams, certain forms of mystical contemplation, and the creative use of the imagination.

In midlife, one must gradually commence a retreat from the centrifugal force of worldly interests and challenges, even opportunities, and follow the centripetal flow of energy inward, toward the center where integration and the possibility of wholeness, rather than perfection, lies.

For the mature adult, such an interior search is far from a retreat from responsibility or challenge. It is another heroic journey to a different but equally fruitful land of promise and opportunity, a "gaining of one's soul." This amounts to a coming to terms with the archetypal Self and a process of learning who and what one is in depth and what it means to be a human being. It is also a coming to realize "the rapture of being alive."[13] Somewhere Yeats has written: "Why should we honor those that die on the field of battle? A man may show as reckless a courage in entering into the abyss of himself."

Gregory, the unconscious knight-errant, inflated sun-hero, and eternal youth, is about to learn an important truth concerning the values and risks of returning to the psychic womb.

TEN

◆

INTO THE BLACK
ABYSS OF NIGHT

THE duchy is secure. Gregory and his first and only love are married. Everyone is extravagantly happy. Nothing could be better.

However, at a certain time every day, Gregory slips off alone to a private chamber in the palace, where he kneels down and reads the tablet he has kept secretly with him ever since he left the abbot. In prayer he begs the Lord to bestow grace upon his sinful parents. Over and over again he reads the terrible story of his parents' hideous sin, and he weeps and beats his chest. But he shares not a word of this with anyone.

Now, the duchess has a maidservant, a nosy busybody who is equipped, like Gregory's stepmother back at the island monastery, with an insatiable curiosity. This woman shrewdly observes that Gregory comes out of his bedroom in the mornings looking happy and serene. However, at a regular moment each day, he enters a certain private room of the castle for a while. When he reappears, his face wears a mournful expression of grief.

Not capable of tolerating such mysterious goings-on, this servant manages to gain entrance to the chamber and hides there one day before Gregory occupies the room.

Gregory enters and removes a flat thing from behind a panel in the woodwork and proceeds to kneel down and gaze at it intensely as tears stream across his cheeks. He sobs bitterly. He beats his breast. He is obviously filled with the greatest sorrow. After a while he finishes with the thing, returns it to its secret place in the wall, and leaves the room.

Sometime later, while Gregory is on a long hunting trip in the far-away countryside, the maidservant approaches the lady and tells her what she has observed. The duchess resists hearing much about it at first, but ultimately she succumbs to the maid's incessant pesterings on the subject. Finally the duchess goes to the private room, still feeling hesitant about prying into a matter that her husband has not seen fit to share with her. Then she finds the thing in its hiding place. It is an exquisite ivory tablet framed in gems and gold. Immediately a cold chill runs up her spine. "This is the very tablet," the duchess gasps under her breath, "that I inscribed for the little one so long ago . . . !"

The lady is feeling herself already slipping beneath the waters and within the dark waves of deadly sin. She has been let fall a second time. The sun of her delight has now sunk into the black abyss of night.

Gregory is called back from his expedition, and the duchess immediately confronts him with the ivory tablet.

"Tell me who gave you this!" exclaims the distraught duchess.

"I did not acquire this precious tablet from another," Gregory replies; "it was with me from the beginning, when I was rescued from a chest found floating in the sea. I am not a commoner, as some have rumored, but come from very noble stock. This precious tablet is written in my mother's own hand, you see? She was a duchess."

"Then the Devil's plot has taken us down, destroying our souls and our lives," yells the lady, "for I am both your mother and your wife!"

Now gloom and despair without relief settle upon this couple. The duchess falls into the deepest despondency and fear, realizing that because of this second dreadful act of incest, she is bound straight for the depths of hell. An icy silence descends upon the couple.

But finally Gregory takes hold of the lady and looks her in the eye and says, "You must not lose hope! Believe that there is always relief and forgiveness from God if we are truly sorry for our sins, no matter how great they are."

Gregory takes charge and instructs his mother-wife to put away her stately robes and assume the habit of a simple nun, giving up her duchy, her fortune, and all her rich possessions in exchange for a meager roadside hospice. There she can minister to the sick and care for the poor and the outcasts by the labor of her own hands every day for the rest of her life. In this way she may earn from God a release from eternal damnation in the fiery pit of hell.

For himself, Gregory says he will never see her again. "I will go away to some far-off place and suffer for my sins the rest of my mortal days, a penance unto death."

In parting, Gregory says to his mother-wife, "Sometime, if we are fortunate, God will bring us together again in heaven, but not till then will we cast eyes upon each other. On this day let us renounce the world and all its professions!"

Then Gregory removes his splendid silk robes, pulls on a simple beggar's sackcloth, and departs the land.

Thus, for the second time in his life, Gregory's sublime success and utter happiness have been suddenly blown to pieces by the revelation of his own incongruous identity. God has dropped him on his head again.

For the duchess, it is also the second occasion upon which her bliss has been shattered and her greatest love torn from her. First she had to suffer the loss of her son and the death of her brother, and now the loss of her husband and the loss of her son again.

We have already wondered why the duchess never questioned Gregory about his origins. She had a good hint in the pattern of fine silk brocade he wore at their first meeting, so like the stuff in which she wrapped her baby when he was sent off on the sea. And he must have looked about the right age to be her son. Why didn't Gregory ask any questions about the lady's past? He left the monastery in search of his origins, but it never occurred to him that he might have actually found his mother when he pledged himself in service to the beautiful mistress of the realm. Many of the episodes of this tale are imbued with a terribly naive and simple-minded unknowing. There is an unconscious and veritable stupidity in their bliss.

This blind and unknowing optimism is inevitably compensated by the fisherman's wife who was so curious about Gregory's origins, and then by the duchess's chambermaid, who was equally curious about Gregory's concealed grief. Every paradise has its serpent. These two peasant women seem to be apt incarnations of such a wily spirit, which puts an abrupt end to credulous and unsuspecting contentment.

Both these meddling women occupy positions of servitude in relation to masculine authority. The fisherman's wife had to do his bidding by raising a seventh child, not her own, because her husband and the abbot ordered it. The chambermaid is a menial servant on the young duke's household staff. Both these women appear in an unfavorable light, but truth, and the overall evolution of our story, are on their side. Their serpentine curiosity sees straight to the heart of the matter and ferrets out the naive and unconscious innocence in human nature. Young Gregory could have used a dose of this much earlier. If only he had a firmer grip on it in himself!

Such cunning feminine curiosity usually rears its ugly head under those circumstances where some kind of complacent masculine dominion does an injustice to the world of the feminine.

In the very beginning of our tale, the old duke refused to marry his daughter to an eligible man. Apparently he wanted to hang on to her. His own wife was dead. Perhaps he felt his daughter to be a substitute for her. This was the beginning of the incestuous tendency in our tale.

Much of the difficulties in the tale stem from the old duke's failure to relinquish control over his daughter's life. After his death, the son continued the domination in a primitive way, by forcing his erotic attentions on his sister, and then, after their trouble was discovered, they uncritically submitted themselves to the old duke's counselor.

These curious peasant women are reacting to the male domination. They represent, at a primitive level, a counteraction of the deeper, more organic feminine world of instinctive nature, growth, and wisdom, which has been manipulated by masculine culture and consciousness.

Both women want to know who he is and what he is about. In each instance, these women push Gregory out of his comfortable and unknowing bliss and send him on the next leg of his journey through life. Their brand of wisdom is certainly a painful one. This is one reason why men are so afraid of women who won't stop asking questions and why men resist too much intimacy with them. Men are imbued with a great fear of knowing very much of the truth about themselves.

Psychologically, such women represent a kind of gnawing and intuitive doubt that enters the mind and seems to say, "This is simply too good to be true."

A certain kind of glorious well-being is simply not meant to last. If it did, then we would be cheated out of the next creative stage of our development. Every time a new "heaven" is in the wings, a "hell" must come first. Like Dante in *The Divine Comedy*, we must periodically travel down through the dark underworld of our pain, suffering, depression, violence, selfishness, vanity, and pride, and acknowledge our shadow sides, before we have any right to enjoy some of the wholeness and rapture of heaven. Otherwise, our "bliss" is just a neurotic inflation, a form of grandiose delusion. Much of our happiness nowadays is this kind of unearned "high." Without our traditional religious symbols, we can no longer separate the archetypal from the personal.

Happiness seems to be the by-product of being tuned in to the psychological needs of a certain stage of life. Attempting to force happiness or keep it in our grip has the effect of arresting our development. A certain amount of pain and frustration is simply necessary for the continued unfolding of our psychological growth. Bad feelings are as important and as valuable as good feelings.

In Goethe's *Faust*, the hero makes a wager for his soul with Mephistopheles, the Devil. In exchange, the Devil will give Faust a taste of life's excitement and pleasure. Faust pledges:

> If I be quieted with a bed of ease,
> Then let that moment be the end of me!
> If ever flattering lies of yours can please
> And sooth my soul to self-sufficiency,
> And make me one of pleasure's devotees,
> Then take my soul, for I desire to die:
> And that's a wager!

Mephisto replies:

> Done!

To which Faust answers:

> If to the fleeting hour I say
> "Remain, so fair thou art, remain!"
> Then bind me with your fatal chain,
> For I will perish on that day.
> 'Tis I for whom the bell shall toll,
> Then you are free, your service done.

For me the clock shall fail, to ruin run,
And timeless night descend upon my soul.

And Mephisto concludes:

This shall be held in memory, beware![1]

In a certain respect, Gregory is in the same situation as Faust. Faust had made a wager with Mephistopheles. In exchange for his immortal soul, the Devil was to give Faust an experience of all the excitement, beauty, enchantment, and sensual delight of worldly bliss. He never said, "Remain, so fair thou art, remain!" until just before the end of the play. One day in his tranquil old age he saw a vision of peace and tranquillity. Impulsively he uttered the fateful words, "Remain, so fair thou art, remain!"

Immediately, Mephistopheles appeared and claimed Faust's soul for hell. But at the last moment, Gretchen, his lover of former days, who had been driven to suicide by Faust's callousness and cruelty, interceded for Faust in heaven. She was a pure and virtuous woman, and pleaded in Faust's defense that what he had witnessed in his vision was an image of heaven, not a scene of worldly sensuality. Gretchen's plea tipped the scales in Faust's favor. So in the end, he didn't have to forfeit his soul to the Devil, but went on to enjoy the bliss of heaven after he died.

Gretchen's plea suggests that there is indeed a difference between our vulgar sensual fantasies—our idle, wish-fulfilling daydreams—on the one hand, and on the other, the fully conscious, responsible, and noble use of the creative imagination that may prefigure the goal of wholeness and inspire our hearts and minds to new levels of development.

Although Gregory "remains" with his fair wife and kingdom, he continues his ordeals of suffering and grief as he reads over and over again, each day, the contents of his tablet. This saves him.

Gregory is living a strangely double existence. In his outer life he is on top of the world. He has attained the pinnacle of success in heroism and love. He is admired by everyone. He is completely happy.

But then he leads a separate and secret existence, every time he enters the little room where he broods over the tablet his mother wrote for him. This other side of his life is full of anguish and despair.

He agonizes secretly over the shame of being a castaway because his parents had committed incest. He was an outrageously illegitimate child of incest, the worst kind of despicable bastard. He had no legal or socially acceptable place in the world. True, he was aristocratic, but he could never have succeeded to the position in the world occupied by his grandfather, the legitimate duke. He was aristocratic, but his pedigree folded back upon itself—too directly!

If Gregory had maintained his resolve to find his parents and learn the details of his origin, he would have discovered right away that the duchess in distress was his real mother. But if she had learned who he really was, she could never have admitted it to the world. And any thought of Gregory's succeeding her as the rightful duke of the realm would have been impossible and unthinkable.

Therefore, when Gregory marries his mother and assumes the lordly office of duke, he is acquiring this title and position presumptuously and illegitimately.

The ultimate fact and the basic meaning of Gregory's life, the "bottom line," so to speak, is that he is one hundred percent aristocratic and one hundred percent illegitimate. His kingdom, or his dukedom rather, cannot be "of this world." There is simply no place for Gregory in the collective landscape of egotism, social prestige, competition, success, honor, or normality. Gregory is a completely "unstandard" human being. He is the misfit in each of us. Gregory is our *forbidden self.*

Gregory's knowledge of this predicament is why he suffers so much in his private meditations on the tablet. In some very deep and semiconscious sense, Gregory feels that his peculiarly incestuous origin violently conflicts with his role as the supposedly legitimate duke of his wife's territories. He just doesn't have what it takes. There is something dreadfully and mysteriously wrong with him. He is caught between two worlds.

Psychologically, we are being told here that the deepest root of our own lives, the central archetypal source and nature of ourselves as individual human beings—our inner Gregory—is completely unofficial, has absolutely no status, and can have no credentials whatsoever in our common culture. In a certain sense all of us happy, successful, and well-adjusted people are an alien people. We are unworthy of our presumptuous self-satisfaction, our vain complacency, and our "high horse" pseudonobility. We are alienated from the wholeness of our own lives, from our inner center, from each other, from God.

Because Gregory has rejected the humble religious life of *inner* symbolic experience, and has now succeeded in outwardly becoming a type of the glorious and heroic solar deity himself (made possible by the gold and the precious silk clothing), he suffers the paradoxical condition of inflation. He is at the same time a god incarnate and the worst man that ever lived. He experiences both these identities, but completely separated from each other.

A Wisconsin designer who was beginning to write dreamt:

> I am in a bar telling an acquaintance how discouraged I am—that I think I'll just give up on designing and writing. The other fellow says, "Oh, what a shame. You could be a 'Three-Star Nobel!'"

In the dreamer's associations, "three-star" is the most glamorous rating in the international Michelin guide to great restaurants. "Nobel," of course, refers to the renowned Nobel Prize. This dreamer met his inflation face to face over cocktails.

This is exactly how we encounter psychological inflation in our lives. Part of us is identified with an archetypal reality, and this makes us feel great—on top of the world, in a good mood, full of exaggerated confidence and uncritical optimism. Our ego-personality is blown up like a balloon, a thousand times bigger than it should be. It is filled with all manner of imperious and arrogant hogwash, of which we are totally unconscious. But just as suddenly, everything can flip over, and we feel a supreme lack of success, secret doubts, and the nagging worry of a typical Woody Allen character, that maybe our success and self-worth is just in our imagination. It'll only be a matter of time before everyone discovers what a fraud we are.

Gregory's glorious "outwardness" is a superb characteristic of effete patriarchy. The demands of inflated masculinity are dependent upon inner psychic resources, upon the maternal attentions of actual women, and upon the secure domestic environment of home and family solidarity. Yet pretentious masculinity relentlessly maintains the phony illusion of vigorous independence, self-mastery, and unquestionable authority. Like the solar deity, Gregory believes himself to be free and independent of Mother Earth, not recognizing that he owes the very source of his umbilical support to her, the unrecognized and devalued psychic ground of his being. So the anima-psyche, in a flagrant attempt to dethrone his macho majesty and bring him down to mundane reality, plagues him with nightmarish doubts and fears. He is beset with inflationary mood swings from high to low, from robust self-aggrandizement to the most horrific misgivings about the adequacy of his importance and performance.

Neither of these exaggerated extremes is healthy, accurate, or true. What is true is that we are just ourselves, plain and simple, no more and no less. Whenever we begin to feel like celebrities, either in a grandiosely positive way or in the negative form of intense and colossal inferiority, we should search out the inflation in ourselves and give away our presumption—rid ourselves of it as quickly as possible. When a patient comes in and ruminates over how inferior he feels or how low his self-esteem is, I may shout at him, "Who the hell do you think you are, anyway?"

Whenever we dream that we are in high places or flying in the air, or of being on intimate personal terms with a mythological figure, a celebrity from public life, or a famous entertainer, we are inflated.

There is an ironic psychological law that says we need some moderate inflation to gain the lavish confidence to go out and achieve something of worth. But that same inflation is both unrealistic and full of pride. Sooner or later we must pay the price for it.

The mother-psyche will indeed transform masculine consciousness one way or the other, even if she must bring him down to the black pit of hopeless despair in order to accomplish it.

It was Jung's insight that we grow closer to God or the Self by first identifying with this central archetype and then suffering the pain and alienation of dissociation from it. This, then, gives us the opportunity of eventually being related to archetypal reality in a conscious manner, rather than identifying our ego consciousness directly with divine levels. Often, the sign of an approaching new and more profound relation to God or the Self is the onset of self-doubts, vague anxiety, and depression. In this way, the ego is being prepared to relate safely to archetypal reality without childish arrogance and pretentiousness.

When people come to me in my practice and tell me how awful they feel, I also say, "Try to feel as terrible about yourself as you can. Then cut it precisely in half and believe it." I hope to startle them out of their inflation. We are indeed capable of refusing our grandiosity, coming down to earth, practicing some humility (from *humus*, Latin for "earth" or "ground"), and living together as plain mortals. Robert Johnson once shared with me his observation that today there seem to be fewer and fewer human-sized men and women.

Every one of us must experience the "Fall of Man" in ourselves psychologically, and come to accept and really acknowledge our human limitations. We must renounce our pretensions before we can make a legitimate claim on bliss.

So, in the end, Gregory takes off his illegitimate clothing and gives up his position as duke. He puts on the identity of "nobody." He renounces the "world" to meet God in his statusless condition as a homeless beggar.

ELEVEN

ALONE

GREGORY rejects ease and comfort of every sort and travels toward the untrodden wilderness. He fords streams rather than using bridges. He wanders the forest barefoot as he fasts and prays. If he encounters people on the road, he goes another way rather than traveling in their company. Whenever he has a choice between a broad, pleasant path and a trackless waste, he veers into the wild. Finally, after three days, a barely discernible path leads him down toward the sea, where, in complete isolation, he discovers the tiny hut of a lone fisherman and his wife.

No sooner has Gregory encountered this peasant than he is deluged with abusive accusations. One glance at the handsome and well-fed young man and the fisherman shouts, "You swindler! You ruffian! You're nothing but a glutton, a rogue, a scamp! You're just a scoundrel, a vagrant! You're a fat and good-for-nothing bum!" The fisherman even accuses Gregory of being a murderer. He cries that Gregory is the kind of freeloader who takes from others rather than working for himself, as any decent man should. He orders Gregory to get moving and not to linger any longer. Gregory accepts this diatribe with good humor and does not resist or protest. He asks for nothing and starts on his way again.

But the fisherman's wife has overheard these proceedings and is worried about this itinerant fellow. The woman reminds her husband that never, in all the long years they have lived in this vast wilderness, have they ever encountered a stranger on the path. Not a single human being has ever approached their door. On the slender chance that this suspicious-looking wanderer might be a messenger from God, she urges her husband to be kinder and more hospitable to him. Having been thus persuaded, the fisherman calls Gregory back and offers him shelter for the night.

Gregory refuses the modest dinner that the woman offers and is content with a crust of oat bread and a cup of water. But after a while the fisherman's suspicions return. He remarks that Gregory's body does not have the rough and worn features of a true beggar and that he looks too well fed to pass for a vagrant. But again, Gregory takes all this in stride, never complaining, even though he, once a lord, is suffering abuse at the hands of one born to such low estate.

The fisherman questions Gregory about his past and asks who he is. Gregory replies by saying, "Sir, I am a man who does not know how far his sin and guilt abound. In order to earn God's grace and to gain forgiveness for my sins, I have come to this trackless waste to do penance. I am searching for a secluded spot where I can mortify this flesh of mine until I die."

Gregory asks the fisherman if he knows of any forlorn and secluded spot where he will encounter no one at all and where he can perform his life-long penance. The fisherman replies enthusiastically that he knows of just the right spot. There is a solitary rock, far out to sea, where no one ever goes. It is a place so steep and difficult to approach that escape will be virtually impossible.

156

"And I have an iron leg shackle," exclaims the fisherman, "with a lock and key. We'll take it, just in case your courage fails you. Ha, ha. It will strengthen your resolve to stay put till you die. I'll gladly row you out there tomorrow."

That night, Gregory sleeps in a dilapidated shed with his shackle and perennial tablet. Very early in the morning, the fisherman's wife awakens him and shouts that he had better hurry if he is to catch up with her husband. The man has already left for the shore. Gregory rushes out of the shed in such haste that he forgets to take his precious ivory tablet, which remains on the ground where he slept.

The fisherman rows Gregory to a solitary rock far out at sea. Its vertical sides rise to form a pinnacle in the ocean waste. With the help of a rope and ladder, the fisherman helps Gregory scramble up the steep face. When they finally reach the top, the fisherman locks Gregory's ankles in the shackle and says, laughing, "Here, my good friend, you may take your ease till you grow old and die!"

Then, on a sudden impulse, the fisherman throws the key as far away as he can into the ocean, crying, "If I ever see this key again, then I'll believe you're really a holy man and not a sinner!"

The fisherman leaves Gregory all alone on the top of the rock, wide open to the sun, wind, rain, and snow, and with only the sky for a roof.

Our hero would most certainly have starved to death, but for the power of God and the tiniest trickle of water that oozed from a crack in the rock's surface, hardly enough to wet the tongue once or twice each day.

Gregory remains barely alive on this solitary rock in the uncharted wilderness, never encountering a single soul, enduring all kinds of foul and oppressive weather, month after month, season after season, until he loses count of the years.

When Gregory abandons his rich and aristocratic station in life and meets the fisherman in the wilderness, he has come full circle to the time he was fished out of the ocean near the monastery so many years before. He is back with a fisherman again, but this time he is neither swaddled in precious silk brocade nor endowed with gold. Rather, he is like a homeless beggar, a person of no account with no proud station in life. He has renounced his title, wealth, and property, and has become a "nobody" again. Rather than being taken in from the ocean to a safe and caring home, even a peasant hut, he is being put back into the wilderness of the sea.

Gregory is now a wild man, no longer tame nor domesticated. He has purposefully chosen to put himself in a state of bewilderment. Psychologically he has gone astray. He has resumed his adventurous knight-errancy on another level and is carrying it to the furthest extreme.

This fisherman with his abusive accusations serves to shrink the princely Gregory down to a very small size. The balloon of his inflation has already been pierced by the horrifying knowledge of his incestuous marriage, and the fisherman is simply finishing off the job. In our lives it is often the case that our feelings of inferiority, inadequacy, unworthiness, and amorphous guilt function in the same compensatory way, to redress an imbalance in the psyche caused by a presumptuous and flamboyant grandiosity hidden somewhere in a corner of our souls. In this sense, "feeling good" is really not so good! "Feeling bad" is often a more healthy phenomenon. It is particularly hard for a successful American to hear this truth.

In actual fact, in the Middle Ages, illegitimate, abandoned, or foundling children often did end up as beggars, drifting from place to place, scraping together a spare livelihood as best they could. When the fisherman called Gregory a "swindler," "rogue," "ruffian," and so on, he was accurately naming the typical qualities of such wandering and unfortunate folk. They had no status or security in medieval society and had to live by their wits. Such people might trick or steal, if necessary, to stay alive.

In reality, this sort of person exists at the bottom of society—and at the bottom of our selves! He lives by a different scale of values and priorities. He has no "reputation" to defend or "image" to protect. By typical worldly standards such a person is powerless, weak, worthless. He is anonymous—one of the drunken homeless or mentally handicapped who wander the streets of our cities, or the town bum who begs for a living.

From the strictly literal and concrete point of view, there is no advantage in being so poor and insignificant. But if we understand such a destitute role symbolically, then Gregory's beggar's robe will help lead us to an understanding of his path to wholeness. We all have a version of this despised fellow down deep inside of us. (Recall the dream of the sick derilect in the subway corridor in chapter 7.)

By entering the wilderness as an anonymous beggar, Gregory has purposefully turned his back on his own familiar cultural background. Having cast aside his precious silk garments and his gold, he has shed his identity as the aristocratic son of noble parents. He has removed his mother-complex persona and entered upon a unique journey outside the boundaries of his family and social station. He has sloughed off his patrician attitude and affirmed his original identity as a foundling. He has acknowledged himself as an orphan. Gregory has reconnected with that important truth about himself, which his mother's precious silks and the gold had kept him from fully realizing. It is precisely this outcast "nobody" identity that Gregory now assumes, as he courageously leaves his formerly happy life.

It is tempting to think that Gregory has now fallen back into his shadow side, represented by his ignorant peasant stepbrother back at the island monastery. But Gregory is choosing the "nobody" identity with full consciousness. He knows precisely what he is doing. There is no longer any unconscious tension between the educated and civilized man and the ignorant and instinctive peasant of the soil. He is indeed much more of a "nobody" than his stepbrother or even a wandering hermit. Gregory is claiming his basic and fundamental humanity. He has become animal man. No roles at all for him.

He is a "nobody" because he is a child of incest, and therefore a sort of "untouchable" in the ordinary world of respectable conformity and worldly status. As an orphan, Gregory is now the child only of God and no longer the scion of his family or culture.

Our tale mentions that as Gregory trekked through the wilderness, he did not use bridges when he crossed rivers and streams, but waded through the water barefoot. A bridge is a product of human ingenuity and culture, a means of artificially transcending an obstacle of nature. Crossing a bridge would have meant that Gregory was following a standard program of adjustment as he traveled through the course of his life.

However, to wade through the water in bare feet, rather than crossing overhead on the bridge, means that one is touched directly by the unconscious and by the deep energy of life itself. To pass over the bridge would be to take an easier shortcut, to avoid a deeper, more independent experience of living. On his singular journey, Gregory is getting his feet wet, so to speak, in living by an original, genuine, and self-sufficient means. Gregory is experiencing life firsthand. In this sense he is exceeding the standard collective consciousness of his age by traveling *below* it.

To walk through the stream is to experience a deep renewal and change in attitude. It is a kind of baptism of death and rebirth in miniature. The Buddhists speak of crossing the water to the "yonder shore" as a means of attaining enlightenment. In Greek mythology, crossing the river Styx enabled one to enter the land of the dead and departed spirits, where, as Homer relates, Odysseus learned the answers to some important questions about his life. Wading through the stream is the "night-sea journey" in condensed form. It is the solar transformation of consciousness from the old to the new day, from an old attitude to a new one.

Gregory has been pushed toward such an ultimate path because his parents were afraid to acknowledge to the world at large their great sin against the moral code, and particularly the evidence of it in their son. They abandoned their child to the waves of the night ocean for the express purpose of hiding their sinful love. They did this because they weren't prepared to acknowledge and accept the conflict of inner wholeness versus cultural conformity. Like many unresolved parental conflicts, this dilemma would rule their son's life.

Until the chambermaid discovered him, Gregory had continued this cover-up by keeping his origins a secret. He had managed somehow to lead a double life, one compartment totally isolated from the other. While his parents could not survive their conflict, his fate pressed for resolution.

Gregory moves toward atonement ("at-one-ment") and wholeness not in spite of his parents' sin, or in spite of his own sin, but precisely because of these transgressions. This is a most startling revelation: that "sin," if consciously acknowledged and suffered, is the way to redemption and wholeness.

Such a perspective is totally incomprehensible to conventional morality. An ethic of the "good person" too easily displaces the unique spiritual journey of the soul and even becomes its idolatrous substitute. Conformity, status, "morality," happiness, and success replace a spiritual adventure, where one suffers one's way to the knowledge of interior reality and a fulfillment of the heart.

Jesus said, "Seek to enter by the narrow gate, for wide is the path and broad is the way that leads to perdition [ultimate destruction], and many are they who seek to enter therein. But the way is hard and the gate is narrow which leads to life, and those who find it are few."[1]

When the fisherman called Gregory those terrible names, he was stating the truth about Gregory's life. Until now he has lived a borrowed or secondhand existence, one that was mediated to him through the silk, gold, and family pedigree. Symbolically, inheriting money or a title is a way of living off the "fat" of the parent complexes in oneself, of following in their footsteps. Any really authentic journey of the soul toward Selfhood must be earned by direct experience and effort on one's own. In our various psychological and spiritual journeys through life, we must all reach the state and status of the outcast "nobody" before we can start our unique quest. A free ride on the reputation, background, bank account, or conventions of our family (actual or internalized parents) does not suffice.

The sibling parents sent their child away as part of a cover-up of their transgression. Psychologically, this was an act of denial and repression. They tried to push the whole ugly presumptuous business back into the unconscious. But the peasant fishermen near the monastery plucked the baby out of the ocean. This amounted to a retrieval of the repressed or discarded part of our wholeness and its reappearance in the realm of consciousness. The fact that the peasants were fishermen gives them a special meaning as well. We all have these "fishermen" within us, whether we recognize them or not.

It is that simple, peasant level of our attitude that can retrieve what has been discarded through our fear, dishonesty, or presumptuous ambition. It is that basic, down-to-earth, unpretentious common man or woman within us. It is that one who is still legitimately connected to the unconscious. He or she is the tradesman—the carpenter, the cook, the plumber, the gardener, the seamstress, the house painter, the mechanic, and so on—that part of us that is preoccupied with matter and basic energy. Often, washing dishes, cleaning a room, digging in the garden, peeling potatoes, or fixing a broken appliance in the house is precisely the right cure for the typical malaise and anxiety of our modern lives, especially if we appreciate what we are doing psychologically as we perform the task.

The lone fisherman whom Gregory meets in the wilderness is the shadow. He is in a sense the peasant stepbrother come back for his revenge. He will redress the balance since he was so cruelly abused. He was "instinct" who got a broken nose from the heavy hand of "spirit." We Westerners are all both the perpetrators and indeed the victims of such abuse in our psyches.

It is that instinctive peasant, the "hands-on" man within us, that is indispensable to the work of great enlightenment. He is the completely earth-bound, practical, and realistic side of our character. He is neither intellectual nor ethereally spiritual. His feet are in the mud and his hands are in touch with the basic materials of existence. It was no accident that Jesus and his father, Joseph, were both carpenters.

The peasant side of our character is not all there is to our renewed masculine consciousness, but it is the foundation, the earth-oriented basis upon and in terms of which we might achieve a higher and broader awareness. Our transformed vision can never be achieved by abandoning mundane reality in order to acquire an abstract, idealized, or sophisticated enlightenment. It cannot be achieved by violating nature in order to achieve a sublime progress. A famous Zen *koan* asks, "What is the Buddha?," to which is replied, "Something made of wood covered with gold leaf," or "That stick you see lying there." The Eastern side of our human character never ceases to acknowledge nature and sensuous art as the mediums through which ultimate reality is perceived. Real consciousness is always incarnational— "enfleshed" in substantial earthy terms, never ethereal, abstract, or condescendingly dogmatic.

The instinctive peasant in us is the perfect antidote to inflation. Jung used to tell his pupils that God loved the shadow in us far more than our ego consciousness. He suggested that we must stoop down very low in a meeting with this more fundamental side of ourselves, if we hope to find God.

The fisherman is an important mythological symbol. Fishing represents a preoccupation with a spiritual quest, the attempt to come to terms with a deep reality of life that lies hidden below the mirror surface of appearances and of "normal" consciousness. When we catch a dream or a flow of images in our fantasy, appreciate a certain feeling, or practice certain forms of meditation, we are "fishing." When we catch a fish, so to speak, we are benefitting from an interior or introverted form of concentration, and we are getting something of value from our symbolic incest, a meeting of consciousness with the unconscious.

The fisherman is that stable, attentive, and patient psychological process that is intent upon bringing an instinctive impulse up into human awareness ("catching it") so that it may evolve from blind instinctive striving alone—that is, raw and unconscious appetite—into the experience of love and wisdom. And like food from the sea, this awareness can nourish us.

The fisherman locks Gregory in the leg irons, then throws the key away into the ocean. He leaves Gregory alone on the rock, where he lies exposed for what seems like an eternity. In actuality, the tale states specifically that it is exactly seventeen years.

This seeming eternity of deprivation is Gregory's initiation, which will prepare him eventually to become the supreme healer and teacher, the Pope. He makes the important transition from an unconscious, immature, and concrete incest to a conscious, mature, and symbolic one. He is being changed from the son who is married outwardly to his actual mother, to a father (*pope* = "papa") who is united inwardly to life, that is, to the anima. He is claiming his instinctive maleness and is bringing it into conscious relation to the feminine. On the rock open to the sky, a marriage of Father Heaven and Mother Earth is transforming Gregory into a new kind of acultural man.

As Gregory remains on the rock, hungry, uncomfortable, and unprotected, he is virtually "starving" his mother complex to death. He is killing off his dependent enslavement to, and passive containment within, the feminine. Gregory is sacrificing everything associated with such an attitude. He endures with utterly no protection, companionship, reassurance, sex, food, or the slightest pleasure. He is locked in the leg irons so that he is unable to change this course, no matter how intense his desire for food, protection, companionship, or escape.

Instead of reaching *out* by seeking to satiate his desires and appetites through dependency upon others, he reaches *in* by living for a time in utter reliance upon crude nature, and in company with his wishful and fearful fantasies. This enforced introversion brings to consciousness the interiority of his being, which is the reflective experience of the mother psyche herself.

In this state he is shedding light upon her. Another world comes into view. Gregory begins to have his own experience of himself within the clear borders of his isolation. This is the naughty little boy who has been sent to his room, raised to a grand scale. Gregory's "own world," not his mother's, first appears in the severely reduced circumstances of his stony retreat. He is hermetically sealed off from the world and from all contaminating or distracting influences. In this way, consciousness is generated in modern men and women as well by deliberately and purposefully setting limits to the casual gratification of sexual desire and the addictive craving for food, power, security, ecstasy, superficial personal involvements, and voluptuous luxury. Gregory is undergoing an alchemical transmutation of his psychology so the son-lover will become the father-consort to feminine nature.

As Jung has said, "By sacrificing valued objects of desire and possession, the instinctive desire, or libido, is given up, in order to be regained in a new form."[2] Deprived of all creature comforts, Gregory is being prevented from "acting out" his impulses unconsciously. Therefore he will have the opportunity of coming to a mature awareness and experience of them internally, so that they may serve to generate a new and creative consciousness.

Deprivation—abstinence—allows room for the new way to form. Intentional fasting cancels the immature demand for nourishment as an automatic and unconscious biological expectation. It was Jung's valuable insight that when psychic energy is switched off on the biological level, it can be reinvested, or switched on, at a symbolically equivalent level.[3] In this way, human awareness, and perhaps language itself—which makes us different from animals—arises. This forms a symbolic inner field of vision, literally "insight," which is increasingly liberated from automatic emotional and physical impulse. Such an inner field of consciousness is the basis for an independent human will and freedom of choice, which can function without utter dependence upon blind urges and appetites. This is the realization of "soul."

A meditative retreat from unbridled instinctive satiation also provides the foundation for self-knowledge and an exploration of one's own inner motives. "Solitude and fasting," says Jung, "from time immemorial have been the best known means of strengthening any meditation whose purpose is to open the door to the unconscious."[4] The rigorous experience of being all alone with an empty stomach apparently is a great help to anyone who finds himself on the hero journey through the night ocean to discover himself anew.

In the culture of the Oglala Sioux nation, if a young person felt he had a vocation to be a shaman or medicine man, he was led by one of the elders to a desolate spot in the woods or desert. A hole like a grave was dug, and the candidate was required to climb in and remain for several days. The top was covered and darkness surrounded him. He ate nothing, saw nothing, heard nothing, felt nothing but his own hunger and discomfort. After several days of this primitive sensory deprivation, the young individual began to see visions and hear voices, teaching the healing arts of divine medicine and religious prophesy. These were sent by the spirits to initiate the candidate into the lore and geography of the spirit world and to give him the secret means to rescue the souls of people who had been lost there through mental or physical illness.

> The Holy Man goes apart to a lone tipi and fasts and prays. Or he goes into the hills in solitude. When he returns to men, he teaches them what the great mystery has bidden him to tell. He counsels, he heals, and he makes holy charms to protect the people from all evil. Great is his power and greatly is he revered; his place in the tipi is an honored one.[5]

And on the other side of the world, in a far more urbane and sophisticated society, the third-century Greek Christian theologian Origen could say: "Know that within you is another world in miniature, in which are the sun, the moon, and all the stars."[6]

It is upon a lonely rock that Gregory undergoes his initiation or "incubation." In the history of symbolism, the rock has carried the meaning of indestructibility, permanence, stability, and immortality. Very often the rock symbolizes the inner man or the source of spiritual power. In legend, it was told that Aschanes, the first Saxon king, grew from the Hartz rocks in the middle of a wood near a fountain.[7] Referring to the spiritual source of man's life, Isaiah says, ". . . look to the rock whence ye are hewn, and to the hole of the pit where ye are digged."[8]

The rock is often a miraculous source of life-sustaining water in times of need. In the biblical Book of Numbers, Moses is told by God to strike a rock and order water to flow. Water gushed forth, furnishing drink for the entire community of humans and cattle.[9] Saint Paul, in his First Letter to the Corinthians, speaks of Christ as the spiritual rock furnishing drink for everyone.[10] In the Gospel of Saint Matthew, Jesus tells the parable of the house built securely on a rock.[11] Rocks have a particularly feminine symbolism. The ancients called rocks "the bones of Mother Earth." The rock carries the significance of hard matter (from Latin *mater*, "mother"). These are the stubborn facts of basic life, which challenge our capacity for tenaciousness and endurance. The rock suggests the nitty-gritty of our down-to-earth lives.

A large and hard rock sometimes means the indivisibility of basic existence, which resists being split apart by artificial means. This suggests the basic integrity of the psyche, and the fact that, from the point of view of wholeness and integration, the psyche is one in itself and not essentially fragmented.

In Jungian terms, a large rock symbolizes the Self, the extraordinary and transcendent principle of wholeness in the depths of the unconscious.

The solidity of the rock and its symbolism of basic, down-to-earth reality are important in our story. Gregory's sojourn teaches that a rock is a good place to pin down and come to recognize all sorts of wild urges and undisciplined impulses, so that they may be firmly anchored to reality in a most specific form. This difficult process is, apparently, how we make unconscious and autonomous psychic contents conscious, and therefore real and recognizable, but without acting them out and drawing other people into our own psychological difficulties before they are resolved.

Simply wondering about something or giving it a fleeting thought or two is never enough. We must pin down our fantasies and dreams in a concrete way according to the reality of everyday life, in order to experience realization. Robert Johnson, in his excellent manual entitled *Inner Work*, outlines specific ways to take fantasy seriously and turn it into creative imagination in time and space, so that it may revolutionize our lives for the better. [12]

Implicit in the symbolism of the rock, where Gregory is locked in his leg iron, is the immobility of his predicament. Gregory was a type of wanderer, which is the informing "solar" spirit of his life (the ancients observed that the sun seemed to "wander" across the sky each day from morning to evening). The wanderer is constantly searching for something, urged on by a longing to fulfill his mysterious destiny. This is one of the hallmarks of the puer aeternus. Even when Gregory had settled down to a happy marriage as sovereign of his duchy, there was still a hint of his tendency to wander. The maid told the duchess about the tablet, and she discovered it while Gregory was away on a long hunting trip.

Hunting is, psychologically, a symbol for the incessant search for the feminine fulfillment of life in the psyche of a man. He is driven by the primitive desire to capture and subdue a part of nature for the purpose of pleasure, appetite, and excitement. It is still an indefatigable sport of modern men, who often feel connected to their basic masculinity and humanity as they trudge through the forests and prairies looking for game. Such a hunting instinct carries the male far from home on a heroic and sometimes dangerous quest, which has its value. But finally the time comes when it is important for him to anchor himself "at home" somewhere in a permanent and specific reality, if the man is to achieve a stable consciousness and integrated wisdom. This is where the feminine comes in.

In late medieval alchemy, the rock or stone was a symbol of the incarnate God, who served the prime function of transforming base metals into gold. The Philosopher's Stone was thought to possess the capacity of redeeming nature from its degenerated or undeveloped form (saturnine lead) into the highest possibility of evolution or refinement (solar gold). The ascending hierarchy of the metals was: lead, iron, tin, copper, mercury, silver, gold. These metals were associated respectively with the planets Saturn, Mars, Jupiter, Venus, Mercury, the Moon, and the Sun. Psychologically this symbolized the integration and the transformation that could produce a higher and more sublime consciousness out of the raw dark energy of the instincts.

For many a year, Gregory will suffer his unique sonship on the rock of the universal goddess Mother Earth, under the overarching influence of the father-god of rain, thunder, lightning, and sunshine. From now on there will be nothing between Gregory and the great cosmic parents of earth and heaven. As the time lengthens out, it will dissolve to eternity. On this rock Gregory will be conceived and born yet a third time.

TWELVE

GOD'S ALCHEMY

AFTER this long flash back into Gregory's earlier life, let us now return to the present tense of our tale. We should recall all the trouble about the papal throne in Rome, and the ambitious men who strove to gain the highest office for their own power and profit. Then, after they had made a shambles of the election, there was a long wait. They prayed and gave alms.

Back in Rome the two wise Roman gentlemen who had been blessed with the miraculous visions went off to find the man, Gregory, whom God Himself had selected, and bring him back to Rome to be the new and rightful pope. It was said that he was a solitary hermit, stranded on a lonely rock somewhere off the coast of Aquitaine.

Announcing to the Romans this authoritative revelation, the two gentlemen begin their long journey toward Aquitaine in search of the one called Gregory. They enter the mountains, wild

forests, and desolate regions, following their intuition rather than
a map. They search everywhere, asking for directions, but no one
can give them any information. Finally a narrow and barely
discernible footpath covered with grass, "where a horse's hoof
had never gone," leads them down to a fisherman's cottage at the
edge of the sea.

The fisherman is as shrewd as ever. As he receives these well-
to-do guests, he thinks immediately of the opportunity for making a good profit from their stay. Only the day before he had
caught a very large fish. He offers to cook them a magnificent
meal for a price. The two Roman gentlemen, exhausted from their
travels, are delighted and agree to the arrangement. They sit
down to rest a while and converse with the fisherman's wife.

Presently, however, the two visitors are startled to hear the
fisherman let out a sudden shriek as he is cleaning the fish. When
the visitors look up, they see their host tearing his hair, then
beating his chest and sobbing lamentably. Jumping forward, they
press him to explain. The man wheels around with terror in his
eyes, clutching a great key in his fist. He has just discovered it
within the entrails of the fish he is cleaning.

"My God! . . . O my God . . . This is the same key I used to
lock that man in the shackles! Then I flung it as far as I could into
the sea. I told him, 'If I ever find this key again, then I'll believe
you're a real holy man!' . . . and now . . . I'm lost! There's no
hope for me!"

The two visitors urgently press the fisherman to explain this
raving. When he has quieted down somewhat, he gulps his way
through the whole story from beginning to end: How the wandering hermit had come along so many years ago. How he, the
fisherman, had reviled him before he finally rowed the beggar out
to a distant rock and locked him in the leg shackle. How he had
laughed and thrown away the key, which has just now returned to
him miraculously through the belly of the fish.

The very next morning the fisherman escorts the two Romans
in his boat, and after he has rowed them a long way across the

trackless sea, they catch sight of the rocky pinnacle looming before them in the mist. Approaching it, they struggle with ropes and ladders until they finally reach the top. There, after having searched, they encounter an extremely emaciated, shrunken, and destitute creature, whose appearance is grossly repugnant.

The creature's body is so emaciated and shrunken that its appearance could only be likened to a sheet of linen thrown over a thorn bush. Every bone and joint is sharply outlined under the tightly stretched skin. Tears stream down the two gentlemen's cheeks. They ask the creature if it has a name. In a weak and hoarse whisper, they barely hear, "Gre-gor-ee."

Then, choked with emotion, the gentlemen pour out to this pathetic little creature their account of what had happened in Rome and about the great revelation. They tell about their long trek to Aquitaine, of how they had veered into the wilderness searching for the Chosen One, the man who had been elected by God Himself to be the new ruler on Saint Peter's throne.

They tell Gregory that the Lord has named him alone to be judge upon the throne and head of the Church, to reign supremely here on earth in the Lord's stead.

But Gregory lowers his dulled eyes and, shaking his head, says, "If you gentlemen are truly Christian, you will indeed glorify God by getting away from me! I am unworthy even so much as to look upon a good man's face with these sinful eyes of mine. My flesh and blood are so impure that I deserve to stay here alone until I die. The noble manners I once knew I have forgotten. I am not fit for human company ever again!"

After the two Romans continue at great length to implore him, Gregory finally agrees to accompany them, but on the single condition that they are able to produce a sign confirming his divine election. He wants to see the key.

The fisherman now steps forward and confesses that he is the very one who had treated Gregory so cruelly long ago. Then he stretches out his hand and presents Gregory with the key. This pitiful creature examines it with much wonder and amazement.

After a while Gregory is carefully lowered to the boat, then rowed back to the fisherman's hut for food and a rest before the party commences their long journey to Rome. As they approach the hut, Gregory mentions the tablet that he had been carrying when he first arrived so many years before. He declares he must have forgotten it when he rushed to join the fisherman in his boat that morning.

The fisherman explains that the rude shed Gregory had slept in had burned down many years ago and nothing had been discovered in the ruins. But Gregory insists they search, and finally, after overturning much soil among the weeds and nettles, they find the ivory tablet. The men hand it over to Gregory. As he gazes at it, the ivory surface glistens as clearly and as brightly as on the very day the duchess first inscribed it. Gregory presses the tablet endearingly to his breast as tears of joy stream down his hollow cheeks and into his tangled beard.

After resting a while, the three men begin making their way toward Rome. Having traveled for many weeks, they at least reach the outskirts of the holy city. Great crowds of people come out to greet the travelers. The people have heard in advance the miraculous news concerning their new ruler and holy man. They walk barefoot and carry their relics in procession as they come out to wait along the highway.

Many are crippled, sick, aged, or deeply troubled in spirit. They are seeking Gregory's help to heal their ills. To those who appeal, he gives a blessing, which mends them in body and soul. The lame, the halt, and the blind come, and if they manage even to touch his cloak or receive a glance from his eye, their health is restored immediately.

Gregory's procession winds its way slowly into the heart of the great city amid the brilliant pealing of bells and jubilant celebration. The people are dancing in the streets with excitement. The citizens of Rome welcome their new sovereign home, at long last, a true physician of the soul who can heal with a holy zeal.

Not only has Gregory been raised to the highest office on earth, but he has become indeed a type of universal holy man, the healer of souls, who commands the very key to unlock the gate of heaven. A key played a crucial role in Gregory's redemption. In fact, keys often figure symbolically as a new world is about to open.

The following remarkable dream is from a man in his mid-forties:

> I faintly became aware of the most extraordinarily beautiful strains of music, and the music was swelling and continually increasing in intensity. This music was full of transcendent spiritual power and majesty, and I felt its rapture throughout my being. As the crescendo swelled still more, I gazed penetratingly before me into the darkness, searching and searching. Then I gradually saw materializing before me in space several golden keys on a ring. These keys were filled with light, and this golden effulgence spread itself throughout the space as the music flooded me with fulfillment and a glorious hope. I was gripped by the overwhelming realization that these luminously radiant keys were in fact the keys to heaven! It seemed that they had been in some miraculous way translated from their eternal existence to this place in time and space so that I might have the certain knowledge that they were, in fact, real. Now I knew! There is a way to paradise.

The keys to which this dream and our tale allude are reminiscent of the keys that scripture says were given by Christ to Saint Peter: "So now I say to you: You are Peter, and on this rock I will build my Church. And the gates of the underworld can never hold out against it. I will give you the keys of the Kingdom of Heaven: whatever you bind on earth shall be bound in heaven; whatever you loose on earth shall be considered loosed in heaven."[1] The same or similar keys are also mentioned in the Book of Revelation: "I was dead and now I am to live for ever and ever, and hold the keys of death and the underworld."[2]

In the art of ancient Egypt, various divine figures were often depicted holding a special key, called the *ankh*. It was formed in much the same way as the Christian cross, but with an oval loop on the top replacing the short vertical arm. Only a god might carry such a key. The hieroglyph for *ankh* meant "life." The *ankh*, therefore, is the key to the mystery of life itself.

In our tale, the fisherman had locked Gregory in the shackle and then thrown the key into the depths of the sea, where it was apparently swallowed sometime later by a great fish. This is another variation of the night-sea journey.

The submarine world of the ocean, together with the large fish, symbolizes the dark maternal depths of the collective unconscious psyche, that region which is at once the grave of death and the womb of rebirth. In the scriptural references cited above, keys have the power to release one from an imprisonment in the shadowy underworld death-state and at the same time to gain one entrance into a heavenly realm of eternal light and life. Psychologically, such symbolism points to the alternatives of dark, forbidding ignorance and supreme consciousness and awareness.

Consider this further exchange between Mephistopheles and Faust, in a continuing episode of Goethe's classic:

> MEPHISTOPHELES: Congratulations, before you part from me! You know the Devil, that is plain to see. Here, take this key.
>
> FAUST: That little thing! But why?
>
> MEPHISTOPHELES: First grasp it; it is nothing to decry.
>
> FAUST: It glows, shines, increases in my hand!
>
> MEPHISTOPHELES: How great its worth, you shall soon understand. The key shall smell the right place from all the others: Follow it down, it leads you to the mothers![3]

Goethe is suggesting an initiation process, wherein Faust is being instructed in the mysteries of the hero-journey, analogous to the primitive shamanistic rite of instruction into secret knowledge of the spirit world.

The fact that Goethe intended to depict the key as a phallus is obvious from his text. The Greek root of the word *phallus* is related to a word meaning to "glow" or "shine."

Gregory spent seventeen years on the rock while the key remained in the ocean during the same period. Every year of Gregory's ordeal on the rock equates to each of the remaining seventeen gold coins that the abbot invested in accordance with the duchess's instructions.

Gregory must do the work—the inner work—of redeeming the raw material of his natural impulses to make the "gold" of conscious realization. It is precisely the key that unlocks or liberates this deep process of change. Consciousness does not come automatically as a free gift from the "mother" unconscious.

The phallic character of the key suggests that it has an affinity with nature and with sexual impulses that flow from the inherent urge to procreate. There is indeed a fulfillment, newness of living, satisfaction, and pleasure that result from the evolution and deepening of our awareness. This is built into our constitution and is not wholly foreign to its overall design. It is not essentially the imposition of an exterior ethic.

The glowing or shining quality of the phallus suggests that there is a principle of consciousness within nature itself that can shed light on the dark abyss of the elemental psyche.

The underlying or implicit question in these matters is this: how can an instinctive animal like the human being come to know itself and gain a higher awareness? The answer, as I have suggested earlier, is through the process of a sublimating transformation of primal instinctive energy into images of symbolic equivalence. To remain locked in the underworld kingdom of the dead, of hell or Hades, is to suffer the unconscious dominance of instinctive impulses, to remain a blind slave of these surging mood-appetites with no choice, awareness, or conscious appreciation of life. This is the state of being interred in the belly of the night-sea ogress.

The seventeen years that Gregory spends on the rock in the

wilderness, when the key is in the sea, constitutes a deep and prolonged introversion. The total absence of environmental sources of interest, satisfaction, companionship, comfort, or distraction stimulates an inward and regressive flow of energy and attention. Psychic energy streams back to the dreaming fantasy world of even prenatal infancy, to the interior unconscious psyche, and to the instinctive basis of the personality. This is Goethe's realm of the "mothers," the womb-source of consciousness. Significantly, Gregory remains above sea level on his rock. It is the key that undergoes submersion in the sea, in the belly of the fish. This time, Gregory retains a clear and solitary consciousness while the night-sea journey occurs.

The key in the depths of the sea represents the libido energy, which has been deliberately withdrawn from outwardly conscious, task-oriented affairs, inverted and reinvested "incestuously" in the interior psyche. Such a condition amounts to a deep meditation and preoccupation with the realm of undirected and unapplied fantasy that is not being utilized for any exterior practical purpose.[4] The Wall Street analogy to this inversional process would be to order one's dividends or interest payments reinvested every quarter, rather than choosing to spend one's income.

In order to really accomplish this meditative transformation in life, one must conserve a certain amount of energy. One must resist wasting it on idle daydreaming or on excessive, compulsive, "workaholic" busyness. Most of us today are far too preoccupied with what we "ought" to do, with what we "must" be about, to save any energy for the use of our strictly *inner* needs. We are plagued by "oughts," "gots," "shoulds," and "have to's." We are far too guilt-ridden to allow ourselves enough quiet time for inner things to happen. To consider such events of the soul seriously is regarded as a "waste of time."

Some years ago, at the urging of my analyst, I began taking one day a week off for extreme quiet, in order to accomplish absolutely nothing outwardly, not even recreation, so that my inner life could have energy available to it for its proper needs.

The morning of my first, experimental day off, I sat on the front porch (it was summer), and enjoyed a second cup of tea, still in my pajamas. My wife had gone to her office in New York some time earlier. I watched the squirrels playing about the trees and listened to the brilliant songs of the birds. It was glorious. Everyone else was going to work. Some of the commuters had just passed by the house at the bottom of the hill on their way to the railroad station. What a wonderful and brilliant idea it was to do this. Just stay home in the middle of the week and do absolutely nothing! I was gloriously happy, relieved of all my burdens.

I remained in this blissful state for several minutes until my eye caught sight of one of the last straggling commuters as he trudged along the road below me, briefcase and umbrella in hand. All of a sudden a load of guilt and shame hit me like a landslide. A critical and accusing voice within started haranguing me unmercifully. "You lazy, good-for-nothing bum! You're a grown man with responsibilities. Your wife has gone to work. Everyone else is up and dressed and accomplishing something important in their lives. That man down there walking toward the station is headed for New York City. He's going to make something out of himself! He'll get ahead in the world. Listen, Perkins, you'd better get off your lazy butt and get a move on, or you'll never, ever, catch up!"

I was seized and practically paralyzed with fear. I was really frantic! But I suddenly caught myself, talked back to the accusing voice, and replied. "I'm not lazy! I'm doing this on purpose, for my psychological health. My analyst encouraged me to do it. What's happening inside me is every bit as important as the work of those damn commuters out there heading for New York. Maybe it's even more important."

As suddenly as the voice had come, it had evaporated in an instant. Peace and tranquillity reigned for the rest of the day.

That night, I had a remarkable dream. I dreamed that I was alone in the house in the daytime. The fuel oil truck arrived, and I could hear the truck pumping oil into our furnace tank. Twenty minutes later a knock came at the door. It was the man from the fuel truck. He handed me a gallon jug full of oil and said, "Mr. Perkins, I have just filled your tank to capacity—six hundred gallons. And here is an extra gallon for you. I have good news for you. Today, all this has been delivered to you *free of charge!*"

My intense and shameful self-criticism almost kept me from realizing that sometimes we accomplish a great deal by severely regulating our level of activity. I did absolutely nothing outwardly, but gained an enormous supply of energy and value for my inner personality. I was repaid many times over for my one day of rest. The following week I felt like a new person, fresh, and excited about living. I had chained myself to a rock, so to speak, and thrown away the key for a day.

In his modern retelling of Hartmann's story, *The Holy Sinner*, Thomas Mann has Gregory say, as he exchanges the company of his mother-wife for a life-long penance in the wilderness, "So shall I find my place . . . the place which corresponds to this, and shall aby [stay with] it."[5]

For Mann, Gregory's prolonged station on the rock was an analogous experience, on another psychological and symbolic level, of his incestuous marriage to his mother.

Gregory is our development of insight. The key in the depths of the sea is the symbolic equivalent of the previous mother-incest. The incestuous tendency is continuing in Gregory, but on a symbolic and, this time, consciously introverted level, the level of the psychological hero-journey.

When the heroic energy is reinvested in the psyche, a new awareness is born, which has been latent and undeveloped until then. This new awareness is the conscious experience of the wholeness and integration of life itself.

Jung often reminded his students that when such new transpersonal contents pass over into consciousness, the effect upon the conscious ego is one of brilliant insight, illumination, or a saving new idea. This phenomenon is as remarkable in the life of the modern individual as it is in the history of religions.

Whole cultures and civilizations are changed and renewed by

certain human beings who undergo these powerful experiences and retain enough stability and sanity to tell about it.

While the most illuminating, this is the most dangerous point in the hero's underworld adventure. Here the major task of the hero is successfully to free himself from the fascinating grip of unconscious images. If he is not careful, he will be sucked down out of control and into the archetypal world, just as Odysseus, in Homer's *Odyssey*, was tempted to follow the enticing and entrancing call of the sirens.[6]

Here the great challenge is to experience the seductive images of the archetypal unconscious without being possessed or carried away by them. Odysseus ordered his ship's crew to tie him to the mast so that he could hear the sirens' haunting music, but not succumb to their enticing charms and risk shipwreck.

This archetypal level of the psyche can have a powerfully coercive and seductive effect upon consciousness, which is analogous to the habit-forming and entrancing effect of a drug. This may get the best of the hero, so that he gives up his larger task and remains forever in the magic realm, a victim of his own failed, misguided, or squandered energies. It was Tannhäuser (popularized in Richard Wagner's opera of that name), a knight of the Grail, who, falling victim to a despondency about his sins, returned to the magic love-kingdom of the Venusberg, and was never seen again.

A talented writer had the following dream and immediately thereafter became preoccupied with a feeling of yearning and vague but searching desires for fulfillment. The dream had almost completely enveloped him in an alluring and euphoric mood. The usual order of his life was considerably upset.

I am walking in the countryside. It is winter. I can tell by the way the trees are bare. The atmosphere is peaceful. I come upon a house with a garden. I wander in. I notice that this house used to be the house Leo Tolstoy lived in. Now it's a museum and everything is preserved as it was when Tolstoy was alive. I see something that looks like a well with a wooden cover on top. I come closer. Suddenly I feel the magnetic pull from the well. It feels like fate, a powerful pull! I stumble toward it. Nothing I will or would do will stop my movement toward it. It is so ordained. I remove the cover. There they are! A magnificent growth of flowers in the well. They are of pink, darker pink, and red. Some are blue flowers. And the fragrance! I feel overwhelmed, but with a feeling of utter fulfillment. This is what I have been searching for all my life! I sit down on a wooden bench beside it and stare into the well, looking at the flowers, enthralled, again feeling deeply fulfilled. An old woman comes by. She is the caretaker. She asks me what I am doing, and I tell her what has happened. She replies, "You know, Mr. Tolstoy used to sit here doing the exact same thing you are doing right now!" The old woman offers to bring me some tea or coffee, which she brings. And I sit there, feeling weak in the knees from this experience which is so overpowering, but I am gratified at being able to feel like someone so special. I am very happy.

In this dream one may glimpse the overwhelming power of the feminine unconscious in the depths of a man's soul, symbolized by the lovely flowers in the well. These are organic anima symbols. They exert an irresistible attraction on the dreamer. Were this to continue with no masculine stability and clear understanding to counter or balance it, this man would quickly find himself in deep trouble. His life would become increasingly confusing to him, and he would be swept off his feet by a passionate moodiness and a reckless desire. The dream is an excellent sign of his profound creativity, but it needs to be mediated by a strong masculine consciousness, to keep it from sucking him down. Perhaps the coffee the woman offers will help keep the dreamer's masculinity sober and "awake" at this critical impasse.

We might add that the possibility of getting connected to the fascinating power of the unconscious anima symbols came to the dreamer as he was *walking* in the countryside. He was far away from the whole distraction of collective preoccupations (other, anonymous "people" and too much busyness), and he was travel-ing in an extremely independent and individual fashion—on his own two legs. In dreams one does not generally encounter the creative unconscious while riding by train or on a Boeing 747, for that is far too uniform, too "standard"! Profound spirituality is no tourist attraction.

In the symbolism of antiquity, the key was a well-known accountrement of the earth mother and dark moon goddess known as Hecate (pronounced "*Heck*-ah-tee"). Hecate was the gruesome and horrible subterranean mother of death, a symbolic representation of the negative mother archetype. Those who might naively, casually, aimlessly, or irresponsibly be tempted to follow the regressive incest-path back to the mother-womb met Hecate instead. Then they were finished for good.

We heroic seekers must be strong enough not to be caught in the regressive undertow of neurotic longing to be a child again out of fear of life's hard challenges. The key is a way of gaining entrance into the forbidden and dangerous realm, which is locked forever to those with a purely "normal" or well-adjusted consciousness. It is also the means of exiting safely after our sublime business there is finished. The journey to and from incestuous bliss is possible only for a mature and well-founded individual whose eyes remain wide open. This candidate must have a self-disciplined ego that is not afraid to take the great risk of exploring beyond the known borders of the prevailing status quo of his inheritance from family or culture.

In our tale, Gregory first encounters the key after he has made a clear separation from his mother with full consciousness of what he has done. He has removed the rich silk brocade, symbolizing his mother complex, and is now free to make the corresponding journey into the maternal depths for self-discovery and enlight-enment.

After the fisherman had locked Gregory in the leg iron, he threw the key far away into the sea, where he didn't expect it would ever be found again. During all of the seventeen years in which Gregory remained alone and completely destitute upon his rock, the key remained in the sea.

What is the meaning of the fisherman's throwing the key away and thus leaving Gregory absolutely incapable of freeing himself?

To appreciate this, we must realize that the key, which is matched to the lock on the leg iron, is another symbol of the archetypal *hieros gamos*, the sacred marriage. The lock is an analogue of the door to the feminine realm of the goddess's womb, and the key signifies the male consort of the goddess, with his capacity to impregnate her with his male phallic energy.

In this sense, the key is the masculine capacity for conscious knowledge that can unlock the maternal depths and, by so doing, solve the mystery and riddle of life. We might say that the key represents the creative and disciplined use of the conscious imagination in men and women, for the purposes of inner exploration. Employed in this way, it is no longer a squandering of the libido through careless daydreaming and idle fantasy, which so easily may take possession of consciousness in the form of a mood.

But a warning is due here. There is a most dangerous pitfall in the process of gaining knowledge and enlightenment. The key of masculine consciousness may become haughtily intrusive, overbearing, presumptuous, and top-heavy. The masculine spirit characteristically assumes it can exhaustively capture and control the meaning, use, and significance of this mysterious phenomenon called "life." Masculine consciousness (in both men and women) may believe it can indeed crack the code of nature and the feminine. Then it assumes itself free to exploit intellectually and materially the anima side of life. This is a psychological form of rape.

Oedipus, in Sophocles' drama, believed he had brilliantly deciphered the Sphinx's riddle and thought he had achieved a great victory. The riddle was this: "What creature is it in all the world that moves on four legs in the morning, two legs in the afternoon, and three legs in the evening?" Oedipus answered correctly, "It is man, who creeps on all fours in his infancy, walks on two legs as an adult, and hobbles about with a cane in his old age."

With this, the Sphinx, a terrible beast-goddess, violently cast herself off her rock. The scourge that the Sphinx had brought to the land (she had been eating all those inhabitants of Thebes who failed to answer her riddle) was lifted, and Oedipus was given the throne of Thebes together with the widow of its former king, whom Oedipus just earlier had unwittingly slain in a fit of anger. All this was granted Oedipus in tribute for his having dispelled the Sphinx with his clever answer to her riddle.

Oedipus had used his clever brains to displace violently the feminine side of life. He had not brought his intelligent consciousness into league *with* nature. As a result, he was in for a big shock when it became known that he had killed his father, the King of Thebes, and married his own mother. Upon learning this dark truth, Oedipus put out his eyes, and his mother committed suicide. All this was the result of masculine pride and an overbearing desire to dominate life and nature with a grand and clever intelligence. Such a tragic flaw is typically patriarchal. It is pure inflation. It is the *hubris* or excessive pride of our modern pseudo-masculine and intellectualistic materialism.

Since Gregory is locked in his predicament of isolation on the rock, he has left behind the normal and standard conditions of consciousness, with its systems of projection (the "world"). He has been removed to another level of psychological existence in union with the unconscious depths. He is much like the young Sioux who was hidden in the dark hole in the ground until he was visited by his tutelary spirits. Gregory is now in his third womb.

Such holy men are not simply practicing a well-known and easily understood art. They are not merely putting to practical use something they learned in class or from a book or creed. These seekers must learn by themselves through direct experience of the mystery about which they wish to become proficient.

Their training is to some extent an original revelation. They must enter the abyss of the forbidden realm and remain there for a required length of time until their period of training or incubation is finished. In every case, this kind of initiation requires its own schedule and cannot be controlled or manipulated by the candidate's whim. It is, in fact, a tremendous ordeal, which the candidate cannot and must not attempt to control or understand either prematurely or exhaustively. It is something that happens to him, or is performed on him by the archetypal spiritual forces of the cosmos. He can't earn his credentials through any institutional training program or through intellectual study.

One purpose of Gregory's dangerous and painful ordeal is to shrink the infantile and inflated ego, with its grandiose need for brilliant intelligence, coercive power, fame, and honor, and the immediate gratification of desires. Another ego disposition will be formed. The new ego will meet the mediumistic requirements of the medicine man or shaman. He will then be a responsible and caring partner to nature and the feminine, not a dominate manipulator of life. He will be our renewed masculine consciousness.

While the key is in the sea, the ego can make no demands. It has no options, no prerogatives, no rights, no privileges. Our tale says that Gregory spent precisely seventeen years on this rock in the wilderness.

The key was eventually swallowed by a huge fish. The fish has long carried an ambivalent or double meaning. First, it represents a spiritual reality, as in India, where the fish is an age-old symbol for the god Vishnu, a giant figure in the likeness of a man, who sleeps upon the cosmic ocean, dreaming the world of appearances, which unenlightened folk believe to be reality. In Christianity, the fish was a symbol of Christ. The baptismal font was early called a *piscina*, or "fish pond," and the newly baptized faithful were likened to little fishes and actually called *pisciculi*. [7] Jesus had fishermen as his closest disciples, and the successors of his chief apostle, Peter, wear the "fisherman's ring" as a symbol of their papal authority.

The New Testament records that Jesus fed a large multitude with a miraculously multiplying draft of fishes.[8] Christ himself was "eaten" sacramentally as a fish in the eucharistic *agape* (love-feast) meals of the early church. Of the disciples' encounter with the resurrected Christ, the scripture relates, ". . . so he said to them, 'Have you anything to eat?' and they offered him a piece of grilled fish."[9] Christianity itself began its swift and widespread growth in the earliest years of the great astrological age of the fishes, Pisces.

But the fish had other, quite different meanings as well, which antedated Christianity. In antiquity, the fish carried the popular associations of ambition, gluttony, uncontrolled sexuality, greediness, and sensuality. The fish is cold-blooded, signifying that it does not warm to human relatedness and feeling, but is guided strictly by its inherent impulses and unconscious appetites. The practice of Christians eating fish on Fridays can be traced to the *original* patroness of this sixth day of the week, Aphrodite. Friday (in French, *vendredi*, or "Venus day") celebrates the goddess of uninhibited love, sexuality, and fertility! The fish was one of her chief emblems, and that explains the fish tail of a particularly dangerous variety (to men) of seductive water nymph called the mermaid, siren, or (in Nordic myth) Lorelei (Wagner's Rhine maidens). Such images express the alluring and bewitching side of the unconscious psyche that is capable of jeopardizing the integrity and the stability of ego consciousness.

In the Western Catholic tradition, the successors of the apostles, the bishops, wear a liturgical hat called a miter, shaped in the form of a fish's head with the mouth opened upward. These apostolic fishermen are therefore symbolic of the sublimation ("spiritualization") of such a powerfully instinctive energy to a higher level of transformed experience, to the head, to the spiritual attitudes of the conscious mind. They represent the authority of "spiritual fertility," as it were, the stable and alert consciousness as it follows the dangerous siren call into the dark depths of death for rebirth.

Chakra number two on the sevenfold ascending scale of spiritual realization in the Kundalini Yoga of India and Tibet, lies at the level of the genital organs. This chakra is called *svadhishthana* ("her special abode"). The element associated with this center is water. The interior field of its emblem is a water-monster fish called a *makara*. The presiding deity of this level of enlightenment is the god Vishnu in the pride of early youth.[10]

In such a context, we may construe the fish to be symbolic of the phallic power of masculinity under the devouring (compelling and inflating) power of the fertility goddess. Apparently Gregory has been seized by the very impulses and instinctive drives that his parents refused to acknowledge or deal with consciously.

As mentioned earlier, to draw the fish out of the water is to make a conscious transformation of voracious appetite and lascivious sexuality. During seventeen years—"golden coin years"—Gregory is fishing for his infantile appetites and incest-urges. When they are pulled out into consciousness, they will transform his entire existence. The lowest will become the highest, the greatest sin will become the highest wisdom and holiness. This is a psychological miracle.

The secret of this transformation is to take the "I"-ness out of consciousness. Gregory accomplishes this by purposefully sacrificing all attachments to pleasure, comfort, companionship, power, social status, intellect, and worldly success. When the ego is then no longer identical with ultimate awareness, inflation ceases, and the union of masculine and feminine, of god and goddess, may take place, free of personal ego contamination. Consciousness without the "I" may then function in the archetypal or divine pattern of transformation that we have seen in the mythologem of the night-sea journey. One "gets out of the way of God" so to speak, so that the cycle of transformation and renewal may occur.

This "I"-less consciousness is almost impossible for a Westerner to appreciate, for we have all been raised, especially since the Enlightenment, with the assumption that any awareness, insight, or wisdom we might experience is something that "I have" and that "I produce." It is considered a *personal* phenomenon.

However, before the modern period, consciousness was believed to be the property of an objectified deity or transpersonal ideal totally distinct from the subjective awareness of any individual human creature. Plato, for instance, taught that truth was gained through an intuition of God in the realm of transpersonal and ideal forms. Plato would have rejected any notion that truth or wisdom is simply an empirical fact of the world uncovered by our intellectual faculties. Jung's term *archetype* comes to us indirectly from Plato through the writings of Saint Augustine.

We probably come closest to appreciating the "I"-lessness of consciousness through certain expressions of speech: "The thought struck me." "It occurred to me," "I was gripped by the thought," "It came into my mind," "I was moved to tears," to name but a few.

But in what manner does one rightly seek such a miraculous transformation? Our tale says that the Roman travelers arrived finally by "a narrow footpath where a horse's hoof had never gone" to the fisherman's lonely hut. This imagery suggests that the path of individuation toward wholeness is a singular path through the narrow door of individual experience. There are no group tours here. It is no easygoing excursion. Walking on foot, rather than riding a horse or even employing it to carry one's baggage, suggests that individuals must shoulder psychological responsibility for their own lives. In addition, riding atop a horse may well signify the way our Western mentality tends to use its instinctive grounding in the psyche as an inferior "beast of burden," controlling and manipulating it for ego purposes, rather than living interdependently *with* it. A person riding atop a horse is not close enough to the earth for discovering his or her inner wise man. Such an approach to life is too "cavalier," too "high-horse." The simple peasant within us must walk.

As soon as Gregory returns to the fisherman's hut after seventeen years' absence, the first thing that interests him is the tablet. When it is finally discovered, he clutches it dearly. It is like new. The ivory is clean. His mother's writing is clear, and the inlaid gold and gems sparkle.

In his own retelling of the tale at this point, Thomas Mann depicts Gregory on his knees, praying.

> Shall I find my life's black story
> Turn to lustre in Thy glory?
> With what wonder do I see,
> Lord, Thy heavenly alchemy
> Clear the flesh's shame and pain
> Back to purity again,
> To the spouse and son of sinning
> Highly from the Highest winning
> Leave for earthly need where'er
> To open Paradise's door![11]

The "heavenly alchemy" is the conscious transformation of the most primitive instincts and urges of the human animal. The original brother's dark deed of raping his sister and the lustful pleasure associated with it has now, in Gregory, become transfigured into the ecstasy of supreme wisdom. The darkness of the hideous fleshly sin of incest has been transubstantiated into the soul's illumination. The twin brother's phallic intrusiveness has been transmuted into a key to the hidden knowledge of life.[12]

In a television interview shown several years before the well-known series *The Power of Myth* was aired, Bill Moyers asked Joseph Campbell the meaning of the worldwide mythological motif of the virgin birth. Campbell's response was, "It is the birth of a spiritual life and consciousness out of the body of animal mankind."

The masculine spirit of culture, ideas, abstract reason, morality, and self-consciousness comes to our awareness originally through the feminine ground of nature, through the anima side of men and the deeper feminine principle in women. Spirituality is not something meant to be detached from or inimical to real, down-to-earth life. Though it receives its impetus from elsewhere, the human conscious experience of heaven and the transcendent comes to us out of the feminine earth principle, out of the womb of the body of virgin nature. It does not issue directly from somewhere beyond the clouds. Transpersonal awareness or any religious experience must come to us in the terms of our biology. It is a phenomenon of psychological incarnation— literally "enfleshment." This means consciousness.

When Gregory regains his precious tablet after seventeen years, it glistens like new. Earlier it had provoked only guilt, pain, and grief. Now it brings pure joy. It is the very same tablet, but its owner has completely changed, not only in himself, but in his relation to the dark deeds that the tablet reveals. He now cherishes the sins that formed him. Redeemed at last on the correct psychological level, they are forgiven.

On two occasions during the course of our tale, the incest has apparently been accomplished literally, in direct violation of the stringent taboo against any sexual union with a sibling or parent. In both instances the incestuous act was followed almost immediately by a sudden and rude awakening as to the hideousness and shamefulness of the transgression.

Such a transgression is not simply a "bad act." It is an infringement upon the restricted prerogatives of the divine, for whom the incest symbolism is a major defining characteristic. Lucid consciousness—the fire that Prometheus stole, the clever intelligence of Oedipus, the apple that Eve took, or the authoritative wisdom of Christ—is a form of criminal trespass against the divine (archetypal) powers of the cosmos. In every case, some intense form of reprisal is the result *unless* the ego has carefully prepared for this illuminating awakening by emptying itself of self-centered vanity and grandiose inflatedness. This is precisely what Oedipus failed to do, and what our hero Gregory has finally accomplished.

There are those very special and unusual people—such as the Buddha, Moses, Jesus, Muhammad, Lao-tse, perhaps Confucius, and to a somewhat lesser extent the great Native American, African, and Siberian shamans and medicine men, who in their own lives, like Gregory in our tale, are asked to take on the transformative and healing task of a whole culture or civilization. Through their own profoundly deep experience of the cosmos, these supreme artists of living become not only the teachers of the new Way, but the very symbols and personifications of it before all the world. In and through their "alchemical" transformations all our lives come to blossom.

THIRTEEN

DEAREST FRIENDS

GREGORY rules the Christian world with firmness and love, and is renowned for his sagacious insight into the depths of the human soul. His benevolent teaching and his blessing serve to gain a foothold in heaven for untold thousands of the faithful. His standard is, "Allow mercy to lead justice by the hand."

Far away in Aquitaine, Gregory's mother hears that a wondrous new pope is able to bring solace and hope to even the worst sinner's heart and that he can heal the most grievous wounds of the soul. She decides to travel to Rome to seek his advice and comfort. After her long journey is completed and she has finally arrived in the Holy City, arrangements are made for the erstwhile duchess to have a private audience with the Holy Father himself.

At the appointed time she is led into the papal palace to the pope's private chamber. Even after she has laid eyes on him as she makes her confession, she is unaware that the Holy Father is in fact also her son and her husband, all three in one!

Since Gregory parted from her long ago, the duchess has performed heavy penance, slaving long hours day after day and year after year in her little hospital. She has grown tired, frail, and weak. The lines in her face and the sallowness of her complexion make it impossible for Gregory to recognize her until she speaks her name and refers to Aquitaine.

Only when the woman confesses the whole tale from beginning to end does Pope Gregory realize that this tired old lady kneeling beside him is in truth his own mother. It is obvious to Gregory that she has made atonement for her great sins through her burdensome penance and many years of heart-felt grief and physical exhaustion. She pours out this story to him, still not recognizing who he is.

Then, speaking very circumspectly, Gregory says, "Tell us, our daughter, have you ever heard about what happened to your son? Do you imagine he is still alive, or is he dead by now?"

"No, I have never heard," says the genteel old nun. "The weight of his sin and his remorse were so great that I fear the severity of his penance must have hastened his death. It would take the strongest evidence for me to believe that he is still alive."

"But what if it turned out that he did survive," says Gregory, "and God granted that you were able to behold his face again, tell us, would you be able to recognize him?"

"I would certainly know him!" she replies.

"And if you were to see him, would it make you happy or sad?"

"Happy, only! As you know, Holy Father, I have given up all worldly comforts and delights, and have lived for many years as a poor and simple woman. There is no other joy left to me but the single hope that one day I might see him again!"

"Now calm yourself, my lady," says the Pope; "We have the happiest news for you. Just recently we saw him—yes! He told us that he had no dearer friend than you, and that he has loved you always in every way."

"Tell me again, is he really still alive?"

"That is certain. He is well and is here even now."

"Oh, please, let me see him!"

"That won't be difficult. He's quite near."

"Let me see his face!"

"There is no need to wait any longer. Mother, look at me! I myself am your son and your husband! My sins were great and oppressive, but God has now forgiven me entirely. And He Himself has granted me this supreme office of authority by His own hand, that I might sit upon the throne of Rome as the Holy Father of all Christendom. I gave everything to Him, all I possessed, my body and my soul!"

Then all the old lady's sorrows and grief were lifted, and she felt a sublime joy that she never suspected would ever be given her. And Gregory, too, was happy, and kept his mother near him in Rome, where they both served God until finally the days were accomplished when each died at a ripe old age.

Then they became saints in heaven. And Gregory's father too, his mother's brother, also gained the throne of joy, and now they all live happily in Paradise with the blessed ones forever.

What a long way we have come. Our tale says that Pope Gregory rules with firmness and love, allowing mercy to lead justice by the hand. This should not surprise us, for Gregory's life as the incestuous offspring of his twin sibling parents represents a union of masculine and feminine principles as an inward realization of the Self. He is the Holy Father of all Christendom, wed to Holy Mother the Church, a medieval symbol of the transpersonal anima. Together, Gregory and the Church represent a renewed image of the Self, a center of wholeness and integration in the depths of the psyche.

The feeling-relatedness side of life, the mystery of the human heart and of love and fulfillment, and the impulses of nature and the flesh are no longer "defeated" at the hands of an abstract moral justice. The concept of "God" is no longer that of an utterly transcendent being subsisting in and for Himself, the personification of all truth and goodness totally divorced from nature and the depths of our lives. "Consciousness" is no longer that which simply dominates, coerces, and autocratically controls our hearts and bodies. The divine masculine spirit is now wedded to the feminine "matter" of life in a mode of respect, appreciation, and devotion. They have become *partners.*

This inward realization or consciousness is not a product of institutionalization, status, or official credentials. It does not stem from authoritarian dogmatism, didactic morality, or programmatic indoctrination. It is not "formalized religion," nor is it an intellectual concept. Rather, it is a living and organic reality where the masculine and the feminine are engaged in balance.

In the ancient days when the great goddess reigned (from the high Neolithic through Bronze Age) before the so-called patriarchal stage of mythic development, human awareness was the dreaming child of nature, dependent upon spontaneous fantasy and instinctive feeling. Consciousness was mankind's imaginative reaction to the naively perceived events of the cosmos, expressed, for instance, in the zodiacal heaven of the fixed stars, through which cycled the eternally orbiting lunar and solar deities. Truth was the innocent innovation of wish, desire, and fear. People freely gave their childlike and mystical allegiance to the cosmos as they lived cooperatively within the dynamic energy of natural events. This is plainly evident, for instance, in any study of ancient Babylonian or Native American cultures. The macrocosm ("large world") of the stellar universe, the mesocosm ("middle world") of symbolic social-political structures and systems, and the microcosm ("small world") of the individual psyche mirrored one another harmoniously. These three levels of congruent experience were facets of a single gemlike reality. Human nature was at home in a familiar world, psychologically contained and nourished within the womb of the Great Mother of all. Masculine consciousness was indissolubly wed to the eternal mystery of life, envisioned as a

goddess enthroned, the Magna Mater—in Babylonia called In-
ana; in North America, the Old Woman Who Never Dies.

This so-called matriarchal stage of mythic awareness, symbolized by the animal and vegetal totems of nature's recurring seasons of transformation, was succeeded in the Semitic Near East
and southwestern Asia by an Aryan-Indo-European stage of
mythic patriarchy. Its chief icon was a transcendent, omnipotent,
and omniscient sky, storm, and war deity. He was thunderously
portrayed in volatile male form by a belligerent chariot-driving
people who descended with lightning speed from the west Asian
steppes into the Mediterranean basin, and into the region of what
is now Iran and northwestern India. We still retain this masculine
symbol on our American national crest as the invincible eagle of
Jupiter, the Latinized mythic cousin of the Greek Zeus, the
Hebrew-Semitic YHVH, the Persian Zoroastrian Ahura Mazda,
and the Aryan-Asian Indra.

As the furious sky god conquered the earth goddess, evidenced, for instance, in the Mycenaean sack of Minoan Crete
(c. 1400 B.C.), the dancing innocence and playful mystery of
natural existence were violated and devalued. Living experience
lost its childlike abandon and was now exhibited as a tormenting
problem of opposites that humankind was obliged to suffer in a
most one-sided fashion. Spirit was separated from feminine nature and opposed to it as soul against body, good against evil,
stronger against weaker, incorruptible against corruptible, eternal against temporal. Beguiling nature was increasingly viewed
as witchlike. The disarming carnality of woman was equated with
indolence, sensuality, depraved self-indulgence, and lust. For
this reason, men of the patriarchate were taught to keep women
under control and in their place, not only because they were
inferior, but because they were positively dangerous.

The reflective mind was abstracted from the body, morality was
divorced from the rhythmic organic integrity of earthly existence,
and the indigenous physical cosmos was made to appear as a
passively created *product*, molded by a supremely authoritative

intelligence residing beyond the pale of sensuous events. Nature was said to be the creation *ex nihilo* ("out of nothing") of this proud and bellicose deity.

Thereby was achieved the Great Divorce of heaven from earth, and the unilateral subservience and trivialization of the feminine. Scrupulous self-control within a moralistic ethical context, combined with a demystified perception of natural events, gradually mutilated the sensuous human imagination as a source of revealed truth, as it suppressed the guileless freedom of human beings to relate easily and spontaneously. Worship of the Great Goddess in all her varied forms was now viewed as the superstitious and idolatrous nature worship of "heathen" antiquity. Religion became identified with a book, juridical sanctions, and moralistic self-control rather than with an arresting encounter with the mystery of life.

A scientific and technological culture soon had "come of age," but was drained of its capacity for a rapturous experience of living. The program engendered by this patriarchal scheme finally became our own mass society of isolated and alienated persons, hungry with a grandly addictive appetite for ecstasy and intimacy, yet stranded within its inherent ambivalence, guilt-ridden anxiety, and rationalistic mindset.

But one precious thing was gained from all this, namely, a conscious psychological standpoint apart from nature itself. This released a capacity for a development in the human mind of rational objectivity, which eventually fostered the growth of empirical science and technology. The mind of humanity had awoken from its age-old slumber, gradually to discover that it had forfeited its secure haven in the nourishing heart-womb of life. The human animal no longer felt at home in the cosmos.

In our tale, Gregory's long and terrible ordeal may well represent the healing of this cosmic split, by having led patriarchal consciousness back into the regenerative womb of natural experience. And there he sat all those years, like us all at a certain level within ourselves, alone, waiting for the remarriage of Heaven and

Earth, of Spirit and Nature, to occur. Like him, we must retrace the advancing steps of the patriarchate and enter once again the Goddess-womb of nature, the feminine principle of deep psychic experience within the heart and soul of man, yet with eyes wide open, our bearings jealously guarded.

Perhaps Gregory's shocking achievement forecasts the ultimate realization, anticipated by the Hebrew prophets and prefigured in Christian dogma, but hardly lived, that the Divine Consciousness of our Western world has finally abandoned His ethereal, lonely, and distantly judgmental seat in the heavens and is even now lowering Himself to become man.

Gregory's realm is not the outer region of political and social organizations and of collective society, but of the interior kingdom of the heart and the soul joined in mutual love and respect. Gregory's kingdom is the hidden psychological arena of *actual spiritual events*, where the transpersonal human psyche functions like an alchemical retort, mysteriously transforming the primitive impulses of human instinctuality into a conscious living experience of awe and beauty, raising us all to a new awareness and appreciation of ourselves and of our fellow citizens on this planet.

The compassion that Gregory shows to the world is the result of a strong and disciplined man taking the feminine principle seriously.

Taking the feminine principle seriously means acknowledging the dignity and integrity of nature, including our own. It means becoming spontaneously engaged in human relations but not lost in them. It means respecting and enjoying the body with its impulses, desires, needs, and limitations, but not selfishly or addictively. It means *living* one's life with patient compassion for oneself and others. It means allowing time to simply *be* as well as to *do*. Honoring the feminine means a certain amount of acceptance and toleration of things as they *are*, without incessantly demanding progress and perfection. It means experiencing and appreciating life in its small as well as its great moments. It means elevating play to an equal footing with work. It means living incarnationally with one's best feeling and intuition, and not abstractly. Honoring the feminine means making self-reflective experience the acid test of authority and dogma, replacing fault by responsibility, and favoring innocence over sophistication. It means allowing our impulses for action—what we genuinely feel like doing or not doing—to inform our thinking, and permitting the heart to advise the mind. It means practicing love as acknowledgment, devotion, and celebration, and not as addictive codependence. Taking the feminine seriously means never trying to fathom the meaning of existence until we have tasted the bittersweet rapture of being alive.

The cold absolute justice of the patriarchal age is coming to an end with the reign of Gregory as the Pope of Christendom. Pope Gregory can indeed live within us all, helping us to gain an intelligent and realistic appreciation of life.

Gregory is the individual human being in us, not our collective-mindedness. As we said earlier, Gregory no longer troubles himself with self-esteem, popularity, conformity, credentials, status, career, success, power, or conventional authority. He is the "pontifex" within, the bridge-builder between the ordinary ego consciousness of the common man or woman and Supreme Awareness.

Gregory is the "alone" man inside us who is all-one in himself, earthbound but spiritually alert. Gregory embodies the highest and the lowest polar opposites of living, not a man of ethereal "purity" who is morally perfectionistic and therefore devoid of a rich and earthy appreciation of life.

Gregory is at the classic "midpoint" of life, when a person is psychologically at the height of achievement, symbolically at the level of his or her strongest vitality and awareness. We can calculate that, if Gregory set out on his errant adventure from the island monastery at about the age of sixteen or seventeen, enjoyed his marriage for a brief year or two, and then spent seventeen years on the wilderness rock, it is at roughly the age of thirty-five that he is elected to the papal throne. If the solar length of a day is employed to represent a classic life span of seventy years, then at age thirty-five one is at the "high noon" of existence. Such a schedule ought not to be applied literally, but is approximately true, coming earlier or later according to individual instance.

Gregory has been through the entire hero journey: Up into the heights of achievement, glorious reputation, and untold pleasure and magnificent happiness, then down into the belly of the monster of depression, hopelessness, despair, and sin. He has endured the dark night of the soul and has given up every form of egotistical security. Gregory has deliberately renounced power, voluptuous pleasure, fame, and honor. He became nothing, a complete "nobody" alone for an eternity on a barren and isolated rock in the wilderness, with hardly a prayer of being rescued.

Then he received mercy and was lifted up to become the supreme healer and teacher. He exchanged an inflated happiness of the ego, which he voluntarily sacrificed, for a far greater blessedness, together with the highest honor that God could bestow upon a medieval man.

When Gregory's mother comes to Rome, makes her confession to the Pope, finally realizes who he is, and then spends her remaining years with him in the Holy City, this suggests a new relationship between masculinity and femininity. The duchess's repudiated son evolves to become first her husband and then her spiritual father! He must pass through these stages.

For an actual woman, Gregory is the Wise Old Man archetype, an evolution and development of her own young animus—her creative potential.

Such a development does not issue from her relations with actual men, though it is reflected in them, but springs from a "virgin conception" within her. This results from an encounter between her deep femininity and the masculine spirit rising out of the unconscious interiority of her being. This makes a woman "one-in-herself," an utterly free and independent individual. It can also give a woman enormous courage and a convincing authority.

The following dream reflected a major turning point in a woman's life:

> I was in my own house. There was a lion prowling around outside. The house was in the woods. I went downstairs to the first floor which was really a subfloor in that it was partially below ground level. As I looked out the windows, I could see the land sloping upward away from the house and the woods beyond. Although I seemed to be able to see, it was nighttime. Because of the threat of the lion, I went around closing the windows. As I came to the end, I stood before an open door that led to the outside, up the slope, and to the woods. As I looked out the doorway, I spotted a large male lion coming down the path toward the house. I moved back into the room and to one side as he entered the house. He didn't seem to notice me, but went to a side room to the left, where he seemed to settle down for the night. In the meantime I had knelt down on the far side of the adjoining room.

This royal beast has always been associated with the power of the sun. He is Leo, the sun god, and because he appears in his animal form, he represents that archetype as experienced in the realm of nature, which means within the context of the feminine principle. The Greek word for the sun god Apollo, *Apollōn*, means literally "from the depths of the lion."

Notice that the ground outside the house slopes up to the woods, and that the main floor of the house rests slightly below ground level. The house is built down low on the landscape and is resting within the body of mother earth. One could almost say that the masculine principle comes to visit the womb of nature in this dream. The dreamer kneels at the far side of the adjoining room, placing her ego consciousness, her "I," in an appropriately inferior position to the archetype. This dream suggests that the woman is developing contact with a strong and rich feminine ground of her being, which is able to act as a container of the great archetypal masculine spirit, God. I explained to this woman that God was entering her soul in this dream. In successive dreams in which this great lion appeared, the dreamer called him Aslan, referring to the lion symbol of Christ in C. S. Lewis's enchanting Narnia Chronicle, *The Lion, the Witch, and the Wardrobe.*

Now back to our story. In the narrative of the tale, when Gregory says, "There is no need to wait any longer—Mother, look at me! I myself am your son and your husband!" we are dropped straightaway into an ironic and ludicrous realization: the son, the husband, and the father are one and the same. They are the different levels of consciousness of a single reality. This tired old woman had grieved for years, scared to death about losing her immortal soul to hell, and worked herself to the bone to earn God's grace once again. Then she made an exhausting journey all the way to Rome and managed to see, of all people, the Pope himself. She confessed her terrible sins to him, only to find herself face to face with the very product of, and partner to, her heinous sins of incest. Her bastard son had finally become her spiritual father, teacher, and redeemer. A grotesque tragedy had been transmuted to a profound but hilarious farce. What an astounding human phenomenon this woman had produced out of her own body in the naive innocence of her youth! How deeply are we indebted to her.

Remaining ever-mindful that we are on symbolic ground, not the concrete ecclesiastical *per se*, we must remember that the Pope Gregory of our tale is not a church administrator or ecclesiastical functionary. He is no career clergyman. He was chosen according to his authentic vocation by direct clairvoyant revelation. He is a most direct and inspired spokesman for God. He possesses real charismatic authority that produces tangible results, not from a conventional institution, nor from collective consensus, but authentically from heaven—from the supreme transpersonal abyss of the unconscious psyche. In psychological language this means that he is the image and symbol of archetypal reality, a channel for wholeness and wisdom that actually functions in the depths of the personality. He is not something we merely "believe in."

As we arrive at the conclusion of our tale, it may trouble not a few modern folk, especially women, to discover that the supreme priest, healer of souls, and divinely authorized teacher is a man, not a woman. Pope Gregory is a celibate male, and the most significant woman in the tale, Gregory's mother, has no direct share in his authority or position as the supreme pontiff. She remains a lay Christian, although she has made a special religious dedication of her own life.

However, Gregory remains a layman too. Our tale contains not the slightest mention of his ordination or consecration at the hands of licensed church authorities. Gregory's wisdom and command are from a self-reflecting experience of the divine powers in and through nature, not from ecclesiastical officialdom. Gregory is without credentials.

In the Middle Ages, such a male-oriented mythic pattern could be taken literally and applied to life concretely, as is still the case in most parts of Catholic orthodoxy. But today it is increasingly more difficult to sex-link such authority. It is a serious and puzzling dilemma for those of us today who value and respect actual women's need and capacity for professional accomplishment and authoritative responsibility.

But let us once again heed the warning not to take this tale literally. The characters, Gregory and his mother, are not allusions to flesh-and-blood man and woman. The story is about an event happening transpersonally inside the personalities of *both* actual men and actual women, not something in the literal church. Real men and women share equally in the wisdom and in the authority, as well as in the vivaciousness of existence, to which this tale alludes. But archetypally, the masculine authority is always symbolized by a person of male gender, never by a female person. The equivalent is true for feminine wisdom, which is appropriately symbolized by an individual or thing of feminine gender. Religious symbols and rituals are not outward literal realities but point to inner psychological facts. Consequently, they transcend the profane context of political consensus, where the neuterized self-esteem terms of personhood, empowerment, and lifestyle are now the basic vocabulary.

The masculine principle in men *and* women is the initiating principle of highly focused and creative consciousness. The masculine brings out the meaning and significance of life. It handles the "subject matter" and the organizational policies of living. The masculine principle takes the raw material of existence and regulates it, brings order to it, does something with it, makes sense of it.

The feminine principle, on the other hand, is life itself, in both women *and* men. It is the actual, unidealistic, organic stuff of nature, as the immediate experience of things and people as they are. The feminine principle is the bonding between persons. It is a world ruled by *heart*, not obligation.

The feminine spirit can never be fully comprehended by rules, ideals, programs, or abstract theories and formulas. The feminine is the ecstasy of being fully alive and "in touch." It is healing, wholeness, integration, relationship, intimacy, and completeness. It is home, presence, beauty, contentment, and love. The feminine is the glue that holds life together. The feminine is life itself.

If the masculine principle is the authority that teaches truth, the feminine is this revelation itself. The English word *revelation* is derived from a Latin word that means to "re-veil." The feminine is precisely that veiling of the inherent mystery of existence according to which we are beguiled and enchanted by the enigma that is our life and being.

The feminine is the "beingness" of actual life. The masculine is the knowing appreciation and realization of this deep mystery.

Our tale appears to have consisted of a long quest on the part of a young man. The woman of the tale seems to have remained at home, first in her palace and then in her wayside hospice, through much of the action, which appeared to happen *apart from her*. But it is crucial to bear in mind that from the feminine point of view, all that Gregory experienced in his life and finally on the rock, all the magnitude and depth of his transformation, also happened within the deeper and interior personality of his mother, for these characters are not actual flesh-and-blood people.

Gregory *is* the duchess-nun's inner development! What he accomplished was wrought *in* her. And she herself is an aspect of every actual woman's and man's psychology. The sublime transformation happened at the interior level of "Gregory," while his mother was outwardly occupied with her penitential commitment to the poor, the sick, and the destitute. That was the ego attitude and outlook she needed in order for her development to proceed within, like a pregnancy. She cared for these people with her own hands. She was their servant and their nurse. She loved and reassured them with her own heart. She was a noblewoman who had become a peasant.

The duchess's attention to human need represents our own capacity to recognize where we are psychologically ill, tired, or destitute inside ourselves. In this manner we may patiently and lovingly attend to our own well-being, or seek help from another. This amounts to much more than simply the business of extraverted social work. It represents a healthy and empathetic self-regard.

In this section of our tale, Gregory's ordeal is something that the lady's conscious disposition enables to occur at the level of her animus. Her conscious attitude and priority of value in serving the material needs of the lowest and weakest strata of the population (and of our own inner selves) released a profound spiritual development in her soul. In this sense, Gregory's transformation is not a heroic development in a man's life, but a feminine triumph in the inner realm of a woman's deep human nature. This happens when *down-to-earth human caring* is of paramount importance.

Gregory is the rising of a majestic power of consciousness and sublime authority inside of a real woman, which owes its impetus and success to feminine nature, not to patriarchal institutions.

What was required of the duchess was that she give up her inflatedness, and make a sacrifice of all ego possessiveness, particularly her attachment to her son and husband, Gregory, as well as to her dowager rank. It was necessary for the duchess to "dethrone" her ego and sacrifice identity with her Gregory animus, so that he could be released to his own spiritual transformation through a deeper agency than personal mother. This sacrifice itself transmuted a neurotic and retrogressive personal mother-son attachment into a heroic spiritual journey of the soul. This amounted to a return, not to personal mother, but to the great cosmic goddess-mother for rebirth and regeneration: the transformation and renewal of consciousness.

Only near the end did the old duchess-nun venture to Rome, where she lived her remaining days near her son the Pope. At some level in the lives of both men and women, there must be this presence "at home," where there is no need to go anywhere or do anything heroic, spectacular, or worldly. That is a subtle secret of feminine wisdom. It is a real woman's quiet and unassuming genius.

Gregory's arduous quest is something that happens within and to a woman's broad-based and very diffuse feminine awareness. He (in her) brings her to a realization, knowledge, and recognition of herself as a feminine being in depth. The roots of her personality and being go down into the darkest depths of unfathomable Mother Nature, where the sun has never shone and where all is ineffable and utter mystery—the realm of "the mothers."

Though the masculine and feminine principles function in the personalities of both genders, there is an exceedingly important difference in the precise way actual men and women experience these two Principles.

An actual woman is dominantly feminine. This is the realm upon and according to which her authentic awareness of self and world is experienced. A sound and healthy woman must be firmly entrenched in and securely identified with her feminine earth disposition in nature as the origin, guardian, and nourisher of life, not only biologically but psychologically and spiritually. Then, on this firm basis, with her roots deeply imbedded in the ground, all the masculine spiritual aspirations of her inner world may incarnate ("enflesh") themselves in consciousness— historically in time and space—informing and articulating her primal feminine experience. The masculine animus in a woman's strong feminine personality acts as a guide who serves the needs and extends the limitations of purely feminine organic aptitudes. It is certain that a woman's animus plays a critical role in her more abstract intelligence and creative capabilities, as well as in her capacity for strong leadership.

It has been said that the masculine spirit brings light or illumination to the dark and mysterious integrity of a woman's basic existence.[1] In the 1970s, Debbie Boone recorded a hauntingly rhapsodic popular song entitled "You Light Up My Life." It was obviously a love song but tinged with a strong transpersonal quality of the spirit. That is the masculine animus in the soul of woman.

An actual man is dominantly masculine. On this sound basis of physical strength, heroic courage, independence, knowledge of abstract principles, ideals, organizational strategies, authoritative actions, and wide-awake self-mastery, he may be graced by the stuff of life itself, which is the anima or feminine spirit within a man's psyche.

In this secure context, a man's thoughts, aspirations, and ideals may bear fruit in actual flesh-and-blood fact and as an experience of the heart, where he may feel the rapture of living in intimacy, where he is valued and accepted unconditionally, where he belongs to his home, his people, and to the surrounding nature, all of which he serves and leads with his strength, intelligence, and commitment. The anima is the "isness" of a man's life, his home base, the inherent purpose, justification, and motivation behind all his efforts. She makes his life worth living.

Not many years ago, my own mentor, Robert A. Johnson,[2] was lecturing to a group of people on his favorite subject, the Grail legend. Most of the lecture consisted in relating the various episodes in the life of Parsifal, the hero of the tale: Parsifal was born, he did this, traveled here and there, met a fair damsel, fought many battles, neglected to ask a vital question, got discouraged, and so on.[3] During the question period at the end of the lecture, a young woman, well meaning but obviously on the verge of irritation and disappointment, exploded with something like, "Robert, you've spent all this time talking about how a *man* reaches enlightenment and fulfillment in his Grail quest. But doesn't a *woman* have a Grail quest? How does she find *her* way into the Grail Castle in the course of her life? Are we women completely left out of this exciting adventure?"

Robert paused thoughtfully and finally replied (I give you my own rendition as I best recall it), "A woman has no need to search for the Grail Castle in order to gain access to the presence of this font of the Elixir of Life. Every woman was born in the Grail Castle and has never left it since. She is the most intimate guardian and ministrant to that inexhaustible cornucopia of life. She is ever with it, ever bound up with it, though she may from time to time lose sight of this fact. Because a woman never leaves the Grail Castle, she keeps a sense of beauty, connectedness, and at-homeness in the universe that a man does not have."[4]

I believe Mr. Johnson would agree that we might gain still further insight by discriminating "woman" from "femininity." An actual woman certainly *does* need to participate in an adventurous quest during her life. She cannot be left out. But the archetypal Lady within her must remain calmly at the center of a woman's being. It is the deep feminine principle, the Virgin Bride, not the ego or persona of the temporal flesh-and-blood woman, that remains eternally within the Grail Castle of a woman's soul, waiting for recognition, awakening, and fulfilling love to come to her in the person of her animus knight, her King of Glory. In the life of an actual woman, this Lady of the Grail is a stabilizing anchor in the feminine ground of her being that keeps the masculine animus within her in his proper auxiliary function as a helpful aid to her feminine self, rather than an abusive tyrant. This prevents her from becoming an imitation man.

Taken in this light, Johnson's reply is a devastating indictment of chauvinistic male prejudices and commands a magnificent affirmation of femininity! If some fail to appreciate its profound truthfulness, it is only because too many of us modern men and women still are bound subtly and insidiously to the antifeminine values and narrowly extraverted outlook of our traditional patriarchal civilization. We have, I fear, still a very long way to go to appreciate what Lady Life is all about.

In the most often performed American play ever produced, Thornton Wilder's *Our Town*, Emily Webb, barely out of high school, marries the boy next door, George Gibbs, and within just a few years dies in childbirth. In the play's last act, before she takes her final resting place in the hilltop cemetery overlooking Grover's Corners, New Hampshire, Emily, shrouded in the wedding dress she wore in the previous act, revisits her life one final time. She returns to mortal existence in Grover's Corners on her twelfth birthday.

At first she is delighted to experience her bustling childhood home again, but she quickly learns that the living don't have time to really appreciate each other or their own lives. They are far too busy, preoccupied, distracted, always in motion. They seem to wear narrow blinders. This realization suddenly overtakes Emily, and she shoots an abrupt and painful glance toward the Stage Manager (a sort of guide and commentator) as she cries out loudly, "I can't. I can't go on. It goes so fast. We don't have time to look at one another." Then she breaks down sobbing.

This is surely one of the most heart-rending scenes of the American stage. A dead young bride and mother stands diminutively before us in her limp wedding dress, gloriously in love with a life she must leave, and now, already painfully detached from it, she appreciates more of ordinary human existence than we ever will.

The lights fade, except on Emily and the Stage Manager, as she says to him, "I didn't realize. So all that was going on and we never noticed. Take me back—up the hill—to my grave. But first: Wait! One more look. Good-by, good-by, world. Good-by, Grover's Corners . . . Good-by to clocks ticking . . . and Mama's sunflowers. And food and coffee. And new-ironed dresses and hot baths . . . and sleeping and waking up. Oh, earth, you're too wonderful for anybody to realize you."

Emily then turns directly toward the Stage Manager and, through her tears, asks with urgency, "Do any human beings ever realize life *while* they live it—every, every minute?" The Stage Manager replies, "No . . . The saints and poets, maybe—they do some."[5]

NOTES

◆

The abbreviation CW in the notes refers to *The Collected Works of C. G. Jung*, 20 vols. (New York: Pantheon Books, 1953–1967; Princeton, N.J.: Princeton University Press, 1967–1978).

Biblical citations are to *The Jerusalem Bible* (Garden City: Doubleday, 1966).

INTRODUCTION

1. C. G. Jung, *Memories, Dreams, Reflections* (New York: Pantheon Books, 1963), pp. 246–53.

2. Ibid., p. 340.

3. Hartmann von Aue, *Gregorius: The Good Sinner*, trans. by Sheema Zeben Buehne (New York: Frederick Ungar Publishing Co., 1966).

4. Thomas Mann, *The Holy Sinner*, trans. by H. T. Lowe-Porter (New York: Alfred A. Knopf, 1951).

5. Peter de Mendelssohn, *Nachbemerkungen zu Thomas Mann* [Afterthoughts on Thomas Mann], vol. 1 (Frankfurt am Main: Fisher Verlag, 1982), pp. 232–33. The somewhat free translation was provided by Dr. Frank Bertoldi.

6. Joseph Campbell, *Myths to Live By* (New York: Viking Press, 1972), p. 14.

7. C. G. Jung, *Psychological Types*, CW 6, p. 445.

8. Luke 9:24.

9. C. G. Jung, *Two Essays on Analytical Psychology*, CW 7, pp. 186–209.

10. As expressed by the title of Leonard Shengold's *Soul Murder: The Effects of Childhood Abuse and Deprivation* (New Haven: Yale University Press, 1989).

11. Oswald Spengler, *The Decline of the West* [1918–1922], abridged ed. by

Helmut Werner, from a translation by Charles Francis Atkinson (New York: Alfred A. Knopf, 1962), pp. 136–37.

12. Ibid., p. 137.

CHAPTER ONE: GOD'S OWN MAN

1. Matthew 22:21.
2. See Jung, *Two Essays on Analytical Psychology*, CW 7, p. 155.
3. Jung, *Civilization in Transition*, CW 10, p. 256f.
4. Richard J. Finneran (ed.), *The Poems of W. B. Yeats* (New York: Macmillan Publishing Co., 1983), p. 187.
5. Matthew 16:18.
6. Genesis 28:10–19.

CHAPTER TWO: INCEST

1. See, for instance, Brown, *Adult Children of Alcoholics in Treatment*; Janet Woititz, *Adult Children of Alcoholics*; and Al-anon's Fourth Step Inventory, entitled *Blueprint for Progress*.
2. Genesis 20:12. Abraham's wife, Sarah, was the daughter of Abraham's father, though not of his mother.
3. Genesis 21:2.
4. C. G. Jung, "The Psychology of the Transference," in *The Practice of Psychotherapy*, CW 16, p. 213, fig. 2.
5. Finneran (ed.), *The Poems of Yeats*, p. 187.

CHAPTER THREE: LOVE

1. Genesis 2:7 and 2:18ff. The other account, Genesis 1:26–27, suggests that man and woman were created simultaneously.

CHAPTER FOUR: THE COVER-UP

1. See C. G. Jung, *The Archetypes and the Collective Unconscious*, CW 9i, pp. 170–71.
2. Mark 12:10.
3. Mark 9:47.

4. James Hastings, ed., *Encyclopedia of Religion and Ethics* (Edinburgh: T. & T. Clark, 1908), vol. 1, pp. 4–7; Vol. 3, pp. 539–40; vol. 5, p. 600.

CHAPTER FIVE: LOVE AND DEATH

1. See M. Esther Harding, *The Way of All Women* (New York & Toronto: Longmans Green, 1934), chap. 2. (Reprint, Boston: Shambhala Publications, 1990.)

2. See Erich Neumann, *The Great Mother*, 2d ed. (Princeton: Princeton University Press, Bollingen Foundation, 1963), p. 175.

3. The period referred to is c. 3200 B.C.–1400 B.C., and the cultures range from the Near East to the Mediterranean region c. 3200 B.C.–1400 B.C. (Babylonian Sumer and Egypt to Crete). The mythic and ritualistic influences of these cultures lingered until the era of the Emperor Constantine, "The Great" (r. A.D. 306–337), who adopted Christianity as the official religion of the Roman Empire as he expunged all remnants of the old mother religions.

4. Emily Brontë, *Wuthering Heights* (Boston: Houghton Mifflin, 1956), p. 70.

5. For an interesting presentation of this theme, see Joseph Campbell, *The Masks of God: Creative Mythology* (New York: Viking Press, 1968), pp. 175–76, 187.

6. Ibid., p. 388.

CHAPTER SIX: THE NIGHT-SEA JOURNEY

1. Leo Frobenius, *Das Zeitalter des Sonnengottes* [The Era of the Sun-God], vol. 1 (Berlin, 1904). This pioneer ethnological work, now out of print, was a mighty factor in Jung's departure from Freud's reductionistic materialism. Jung followed Frobenius closely in his *Transformation and Symbols of the Libido* (1912), CW 5, after which the collaborative friendship between the two men rapidly deteriorated.

2. Long-standing mottoes of Alcoholics Anonymous.

3. Romans 6:1.

4. *The Hymnal 1982: According to the Use of The Episcopal Church* (New York: Church Pension Fund, 1985), no. 593.

5. See Jung, *Symbols of Transformation*, CW 5, especially p. 426.

6. John 3:3.

CHAPTER SEVEN: THE SHADOW OF PERFECTION

1. See *Gregorius*, line 1323n.
2. Genesis 4:3–8.
3. See, e.g., Jung, CW 5, para. 581; CW 6, para. 311; CW 7, paras. 111–13.
4. Thomas Hutchinson, *Wordsworth: Poetical Works* (Oxford: University Press, 1936), p. 460.
5. M., *The Gospel of Sri Ramakrishna*, revised by Swami Abhedananda (Boston: Beacon Press, 1947), p. 203.
6. Ephesians 4:24.

CHAPTER EIGHT: THE WINDS' DESIGN

1. James Joyce, *A Portrait of the Artist as a Young Man* (New York: Penguin Books, 1976), p. 162.
2. Ibid., p. 171.
3. Ibid., p. 172.
4. Malachi 4:2 and Matthew 17:2.
5. Among Christians, Jesus Christ has been conceived as vicariously accomplishing this heroic journey of transformation *for* them, in their behalf. Jung's required to enter into a much more immediate and responsible participation in this spiritual-psychological journey. According to Jung, we should actively enter into the symbolic experience of death and rebirth through our inner awareness of the universal archetype of the Self that Christ represents in each of us. We should connect to this archetypal process while we are alive as the central dimension of our psychological development. It is the savior god-man *within* and beyond ego who actually accomplishes such a sublime feat, not someone long ago, an entirely different person from ourselves, who gained something for us.

    Nor was it that other first person, Adam, a supposed actual human being, separated from us by a vast chasm of primordial legend-history, who began our troubles so long before any of us were born. Somewhere inside ourselves, we are both the cause and the solution to our own difficulties. At a much deeper level than our narrow egotism or our inflatedness, we are each instances of both Adam and Christ.
6. Seven is the mystical number associated with the cycle of transmutations and the evolution of consciousness. We have the pre-Copernican seven "planets" that were believed to encircle our Earth: the sun, the moon,

Mercury, Venus, Mars. Jupiter, and Saturn; seven days in the week named (in Latin) after these very planets; "seventh heaven"; seven alchemical "metals" associated with the same planets: gold, silver, mercury, copper, iron, tin, and lead; seven musical tones in the octave scale; the seven wonders of the ancient world; seven *chakras*, or centers of subtle energy in the body, according to Yoga; the seven days of creation in Genesis; the sevenfold gifts of the Holy Spirit in the New Testament. The appearance of the number seven means that a standard archetypal pattern is being presented; a winding serpentine odyssey toward eventual wholeness is gradually working itself out. But that completion is for later in our story.

7. John Julius Norwich, *A History of Venice* (New York: Alfred A. Knopf, 1982), p. 139.

8. See Emma Jung and Marie-Louise von Franz, *The Grail Legend* (New York: G. P. Putnam's Sons, 1970), pp. 79–97.

9. Revelation 19:12–15.

10. John 3:8–11.

CHAPTER NINE: THE SUN OF HER DELIGHT

1. As stated in the Nicene Creed (A.D. 325).

2. Frederick Hart, *Michelangelo's Drawings* (New York: Harry N. Abrams, 1971), p. 83.

3. The celestial queenship of Mary was formally set forth in the dogma of her Bodily Assumption into Heaven, declared officially in 1950 by Pope Pius XII (Apostolic Constitution, "Munificentissimus Deus," Sections 22–23) but unofficially held as a pious opinion since relatively early times. In this context, Mary, as the Mother and Bride (Sponsa) of God, is nuptially united to the Godhead as Divine Groom (Sponsus) in the heavenly bridal chamber. Psychologically, this indicates that the feminine principle is raised to full stature with the Holy Trinity, forming a quaternity of four persons. Theologically, this dogma declares the potential for apotheosis, or deification of all human creatures, with Mary serving as the preeminent instance and pattern after Christ Himself.

4. Henry Adams, *Mount St. Michael and Chartres* (Boston: Houghton Mifflin Co., 1904).

5. Ibid., p. 198.

6. The final words of Emma Lazarus's poem, "The New Colossus," inscribed upon a tablet within the pedestal of the Statue of Liberty in New York Harbor.

7. See Jung, CW 9i, pp. 167–71.

8. An Orthodox hymn to the Theotokos, or Mother of God, from the Liturgy of Saint Basil, gives us the same image: "He made your body into a throne, and your womb he made more spacious than the heavens." The Very Rev. Vladimir Soroka, compiler, *The Divine Liturgy: Liturgical Music* (n.p., 1970), p. 127.

9. Stephen Mitchell, *The Enlightened Mind* (New York: HarperCollins, 1991), p. 30.

10. John Layard, "The Incest Taboo and the Virgin Archetype," *Eranos Yearbook*, vol. 12 (Zurich: Rhein Verlag, 1945): 254–307.

11. The term *Ground of Being* was suggested by the late theologian Paul Tillich as a modern reference for God.

12. Jung, CW 7, p. 135f.

13. Joseph Campbell, *The Power of Myth* (New York: Doubleday, 1988).

CHAPTER TEN: INTO THE BLACK ABYSS OF NIGHT

1. Johann Wolfgang von Goethe, *Faust*, translated by Philip Wayne (Baltimore: Penguin Books, 1949) part I, p. 87.

CHAPTER ELEVEN: ALONE

1. Matthew 7:13–14.

2. Jung, CW 5, para. 671n.

3. Ibid., p. 335.

4. Ibid.

5. Natalie Curtis, *The Indians' Book* (New York: Harper Brothers, 1907), pp. 38–39. (Reprint, New York: Crown, 1986.)

6. "Homiliae in Leviticum, V, 2."

7. James Hastings, *Encyclopedia of Religion and Ethics*, vol. 7, (Edinburgh: T. and T. Clark, 1914), p. 199; vol. 1, p. 350; vol. 11, p. 876; vol. 2, p. 507.

8. Isaiah 51:1.

9. Numbers 20:8.

10. 1 Corinthians 10:4.

11. Matthew 7:24.

12. Robert A. Johnson, *Inner Work*: Using Dreams and Active Imagination for Personal Growth (San Francisco: Harper and Row, 1985).

CHAPTER TWELVE: GOD'S ALCHEMY

1. Matthew 16:18–19.
2. Revelation 1:18.
3. Goethe, *Faust*, part II, p. 276.
4. See Jung, CW 5, chap. 2, "Two Kinds of Thinking."
5. Mann, *The Holy Sinner*, p. 232.
6. Homer, *The Odyssey*, book XII, "Scylla and Charybdis."
7. Jung, CW 9ii, para. 162.
8. Luke 9:13.
9. Luke 24:42.
10. Arthur Avalon [Sir John Woodroffe], *The Serpent Power* (Madras: Ganesh & Co., 6 eds. 1918–1958), p. 365 and plate III opposite.
11. Mann, *The Holy Sinner*, p. 301.
12. Freud and Jung did not understand libido (psychic energy) and sublimation (the transformation of this instinctive energy into new applications) in the same way. Both agreed that sublimation is how a higher consciousness develops out of basic instinctive energy.

    Freud taught that libido is fundamentally and always sexual. In his paradigm, sexual energy can be rechanneled in disguised form to meet the basic needs for infantile sexual gratification in a variety of indirect substitutional pathways. But in the last analysis, according to Freud, psychic energy is still essentially sexual. These multitudinous pathways of indirect gratification make up the symbolic stuff of human culture. In this context, the elements of art and religion are the "sublimated" (spiritual) versions of the basic sexual objects of desire. For instance, when you dream about or actually enter the door of a church or synagogue, this is a disguised experience of having sex with your mother, or the desire of returning to her actual womb. The peace and fulfillment that result from worship in the church is *really* the gratification of your infantile sexual desires disguised and shifted to this higher, "spiritual" plane.

    From the Jungian perspective, Freud's sexual theory is a reductionistic devaluation of artistic and religious symbols. Jung did not see libido as essentially sexual. For him it is neutral and can take many different forms, including sex. Jung saw sublimation, or the symbolic transformation of instinctive psychic energy by the archetypal power of Spirit, as functioning like a hydrogenerator, which transforms water power into electricity. The river current captures the basic power of gravity, then the turbine dynamo transforms this water power into electricity. It would be ridiculous to interpret the resulting electricity as "really" disguised water power. Energy has actually been converted from one form into another. Physical energy that had once been in the form of a river current is now in the form of positive and negative electric charges. It does not help your use or appreciation of electricity to be constantly reminded that you "really" crave to drink water every time you flick the light switch, but are just afraid to admit it.

CHAPTER THIRTEEN: DEAREST FRIENDS

1. Irene Claremont de Castellejo, *Knowing Woman: A Feminine Psychology* (New York: G. P. Putnam's Sons, 1973), p. 84f.

2. Author of *He, She, We, Inner Work, Ecstasy, Femininity Lost and Regained, Transformation*, and *Owning Your Own Shadow.*

3. See Robert W. Linker, *Chretien de Troyes: The Story of the Grail* (Chapel Hill: University of North Carolina Press, 1952). This edition is out of print, but there is a paperback version of this Parsifal tale: Chretien de Troyes, *The Story of the Grail; or, Perceval*, edited by Robert T. Pickens. Translated by William W. Kibler (Hamden, Conn.: Garland Publishing, 1990).

4. See Robert Johnson, *He*, rev. ed. (New York: Harper & Row, 1989), p. 55.

5. Thornton Wilder, *Our Town: A Play in Three Acts*, acting ed. (New York: Coward-McCann/Samuel French, 1938, 1939), pp. 82–83 and 108 (costume plot).

INDEX

Index